DINOSAURS
and Other Archosaurs

The RANDOM HOUSE
LIBRARY OF KNOWLEDGE™

WRITTEN AND ILLUSTRATED
BY Peter Zallinger

RANDOM HOUSE   NEW YORK

DINOSAURS
AND OTHER ARCHOSAURS

*Dedicated to the memory of
David Hemingway Parsons, 1926–1985*

The author wishes to thank the following people for their assistance in the preparation of this book: Dr. John H. Ostrom, Curator of Vertebrate Paleontology, Peabody Museum of Natural History, Yale University, New Haven, Connecticut; Dr. Leo J. Hickey, Director and Curator of Paleobotany, Peabody Museum of Natural History, Yale University; Robert Allen, Chief Preparator of Vertebrate Paleontology, Peabody Museum of Natural History, Yale University; Dr. J. David Archibald, Department of Zoology, San Diego State University, San Diego, California; Dr. Peter Galton, Department of Biology, University of Bridgeport, Bridgeport, Connecticut; John Horner, Curator of Vertebrate Paleontology, Museum of the Rockies, Montana State University, Bozeman, Montana; Dr. Wann Langston, Jr., Director, Vertebrate Paleontology Laboratory, Texas Memorial Museum, University of Texas, Austin, Texas; Dr. Kevin Padian, Curator, Museum of Paleontology, University of California, Berkeley, California; Dr. Bruce H. Tiffney, Curator of Herbarium and Paleobotanical Collections, Peabody Museum of Natural History, Yale University; and Jean Day Zallinger, illustrator, North Haven, Connecticut.

Library of Congress Cataloging-in-Publication Data:
Zallinger, Peter.
  Dinosaurs and other archosaurs.
  (The Random House library of knowledge ; 6)
  Includes index.
  SUMMARY: Surveys the dinosaurs and other smaller prehistoric reptiles and describes many individual species.
  1. Dinosaurs—Juvenile literature. 2. Squamata, Fossil—Juvenile literature. [1. Dinosaurs. 2. Prehistoric animals] I. Title. II. Series.
QE862.D5Z35   1986   567.9′1   85-42930
ISBN: 0-394-84421-1 (trade); 0-394-94421-6 (lib. bdg.)

Manufactured in the United States of America
1   2   3   4   5   6   7   8   9   0

CONTENTS

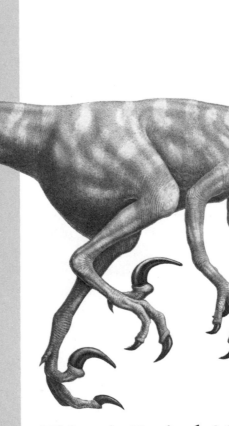

Triassic Period 23

FOREWORD

THERE ARE NO DINOSAURS living today. Yet no one questions the fact that dinosaurs once lived—and that they came in many shapes and sizes. We are told that, as a group, dinosaurs were very successful for more than 140 million years, living on all the continents of the earth (though none have yet been found in Antarctica), and were adapted to a wide variety of living conditions. Dinosaurs clearly were the "royal family" of the Archosaurs, those reptiles that most experts consider more anatomically advanced than reptiles such as turtles, lizards, and snakes. Archosaurs include the crocodiles and alligators that live today, as well as all dinosaurs, their ancestors the thecodonts, and flying reptiles called pterosaurs, all of which are extinct. It may surprise you to know that many scientists believe that birds are closely related to the Archosaurs. You will be even more surprised to learn that some scientists believe birds arose directly from the dinosaurs. That, you say, cannot be true. We know that the dinosaurs became extinct about 65 million years ago without leaving any descendants.

You are right: that is what we have been taught—and for many years it has been a widely accepted theory. But recent studies have raised some doubts, and lucky for me I have been a part of stimulating those doubts. My studies of the oldest known fossil bird, *Archaeopteryx,* and those of some of the carnivorous dinosaurs, especially *Deinonychus* and its relatives *Ornitholestes* and *Compsognathus,* have convinced me that *Archaeopteryx* evolved directly from that group of dinosaurs. In fact, some scientists who agree go even one step further. They say that *Archaeopteryx* was not only a bird—it was also a "feathered dinosaur." Even though *Archaeopteryx* lived at the peak of the dinosaur era about 150 million years ago, I am not quite ready to go that far.

Today, a controversy still continues over whether birds are closely related to the carnivorous dinosaurs or to some other kind of animal. Some scientists suggest that they arose from the dinosaur ancestors, the thecodonts. Others argue that bird ancestors were close to the crocodiles. *Archaeopteryx* may or may not be the direct ancestor of modern birds, but few doubt that it was a bird. Most scientists agree that it also was very similar to some of the carnivorous dinosaurs—particularly those kinds we call coelurosaurs. This controversy illustrates one of the most important reasons for continuing our search for more fossils, more specimens of *Archaeopteryx*—to help us decide which hypothesis is the correct one.

As a working paleontologist, I can tell you what this task involves. Finding the important relevant evidence means focusing our search. For example, *Archaeopteryx* lived during the late part of the Jurassic period. Therefore we must concentrate future expeditions in those regions of the world where sedimentary rocks of Late Jurassic age are still preserved. The next step is to decide which of those areas is most likely to have preserved the critical fossil remains. Having selected one area—say, southeastern Wyoming—the next task is to organize the expedition. We select the proper number and right kind of participants: experts in geology with an understanding of rocks; prospectors with keen eyes for spotting the exposed fossil fragments; worker-collectors willing to dig with pick and shovel to quarry out the fossils; packers skilled at packaging and protecting the delicate fossils for transport back to the museum laboratory; and, last but not least, a good camp cook to keep everyone happy. Remember that such fossil remains are rarely found next door to the museum—they always seem to occur in the most remote wilderness, where they often must be carried great distances by backpack to the nearest truck or field van.

A discovery has been made! I see bone fragments on the side of that badland hill over there. My assistant Grant Meyer and I rush to the spot. The fragments are well-preserved and are immediately identifiable as the claws and hand bones of a small carnivorous dinosaur. This was one of my most important discoveries—the finding of *Deinonychus*. Unfortunately, that afternoon in 1964, we were not properly equipped for a major excavation job, and so were limited to retrieving just the exposed fragments and those bones buried just below the surface. Further excavation had to wait until next summer's expedition. For the next several years, Yale expeditions returned each summer to the *Deinonychus* site. Each year, with great care we excavated hundreds of the fragile bones of this strangest of dinosaurs. Those remains were carefully wrapped and returned to my laboratories at Yale, where they were unwrapped and prepared by skilled specialists at the Peabody Museum. When everything was finally removed from the enclosing rock, we all recognized that this had been a most unusual animal. In some ways it resembled certain dinosaurs that we already knew about—but in other ways it was very different from anything that had been found before. For one thing, this animal had a large sharp claw on each hind foot—a strongly curved claw for killing its prey. That distinctive feature caused me to give this new animal the name *Deinonychus* which means "terrible claw." You can see on pages 62–63 how artist Peter Zallinger thinks this creature may have looked.

Deinonychus was a very lucky find for me in more ways than one. It was not the first—or the last—discovery, but it gave me new evidence about a kind of animal that we had not known before. And because of its unusual anatomy, it made some of us think a lot more than we had before about what strange animals dinosaurs might have been: how they lived and what their biology might have been like. For example, the anatomy of *Deinonychus,* an animal that could run only on its hind legs—not on all fours—convinced me that this creature and perhaps certain other dinosaurs closely related to *Deinonychus* must have been extremely active animals—like birds and many mammals around us today. Why did I conclude this? Because of that terrible claw on its hind feet—feet otherwise used for walking, running, or leaping on its prey. But with those claws, *Deinonychus* must also have killed.

That speculation led to the strong suspicion that *Deinonychus* and perhaps other dinosaurs were not cold-blooded like living crocodiles, lizards, and turtles, but might have been warm-blooded like modern birds and mammals—and thus capable of intense activity. How could we test that suspicion? Not by experiments with living dinosaurs, because we know that there are none. Only by exploring for more dinosaur specimens and then by carefully studying their remains. We must search on; our curiosity demands answers. So expeditions go out nearly every year from such institutions as the British Museum in London; the Soviet Academy of Sciences in Russia; the Paleontological Institute in China; the American Museum in New York City; and the Smithsonian Institution in Washington, D.C.—and on occasion from my own museum, the Peabody Museum at Yale University. These are only a few of the world centers that still look for dinosaurs—and have provided the actual specimens that are the bases for this book. Read on—you have an expedition before you.

JOHN H. OSTROM
Professor of Geology and
Curator of Vertebrate Paleontology, Yale University

Introduction

IN 1841, A YOUNG British scientist named Richard Owen described a new "tribe" of ancient beasts, known only from a few fossilized bones and teeth. The remains of these animals resembled those of large, water-dwelling reptiles from the Mesozoic Era (the Age of Reptiles), but these animals were clearly land dwellers. Owen determined that they were adapted to life on dry land largely because of their hip structures: several fused vertebrae were joined to the pelvis to form a strong, rigid structure. This feature, along with the shape of their legs and feet, indicated that the animals were built for walking, not swimming. Based on this finding, Owen proposed that a new division of Mesozoic reptiles be established. He called it Dinosauria, meaning "terrible lizards."

Two Groups of Dinosaurs

In 1887, another British scientist, Harry Govier Seeley, divided the Dinosauria into two groups: Order Saurischia (lizard-hipped) and Order Ornithischia (bird-hipped) (pages 14–17). Subsequent research has shown many other differences between the two orders and an enormous range of specialization in both.

The word *dinosaur*, still a popular term, is no longer used in our present system of classification. Paleontologists, the scientists who study prehistoric animals, now wonder just how closely related saurischians and ornithischians really were. They shared a common ancestry, but Orders Pterosauria (winged reptiles) and Crocodilia also shared those ancestors. There is even some doubt whether Order Saurischia reflects a natural grouping. Not a single skeletal characteristic is found in all saurischians and only in them. On the other hand, all ornithischians possessed a feature otherwise unknown among vertebrates: a single bone (the predentary) joined the main jawbones (dentaries) to form the end of the chin.

Classification of Plants and Animals

Our present system of classification (see the box on the next page) divides Class Reptilia into four subclasses: Anapsida, Synapsida, Eurapsida, and Diapsida, based on the presence and position of openings in the sides of their skulls behind the eyes (temporal openings). Diapsids have two such openings, one above the other on each side of the skull. Archosaurs, the "ruling reptiles," are distinguished primarily from other diapsids (whose modern representatives include lizards, snakes, and tuataras) by another opening in front of each eye.

The superorder, Archosauria, contains five orders: Thecodontia, Pterosauria, Saurischia, Ornithischia, and Crocodilia (pages 14–17).

Evolution of Dinosaurs and Other Archosaurs

The first archosaurs (Order Thecodontia) arose over 225 million years ago (pages 26–27). Thecodonts had to compete with a large, well-established community of mammal-like reptiles called therapsids (page 13). Yet by the middle of the Triassic period (the first period of the Mesozoic Era) the thecodonts dominated.

Scientists attribute their success to improvements in their posture. Thecodonts showed a progressive tendency to stand more erect than their therapsid contemporaries, drawing their elbows and knees in closer to their trunks. They walked with their bodies high off the ground, their feet almost directly under their bodies, and their hind limbs were substantially longer than their forelimbs. Some of the pseudosuchian thecodonts, the direct ancestors of the other archosaurian orders, were bipedal (walked on their hind legs) and ran on their toes.

Dinosaurs exhibited a "fully improved" stance. Most reptiles waddle with their knees splayed out to the sides away from their bodies. But dinosaurs' thighbones were shaped like ours, and they walked like modern mammals or birds. Comparable adjustments are evident in their shoulder structure.

Were Dinosaurs Warm-Blooded?

In 1969, Professor John Ostrom of Yale University challenged the traditional image of the cold-blooded, lethargic dinosaur. Ectotherms (cold-blooded animals) rely on the sun to raise their body temperature, whereas endotherms (warm-blooded animals) generate their own body heat and maintain a constant temperature in spite of fluctuating temperatures in

Every plant and animal is assigned a position within a classification hierarchy in such a way as to express its relationship to the whole. For example, the famous *Tyrannosaurus rex* is classified in descending order of categories as follows:

Kingdom—Animal
Phylum—Chordata
Subphylum—Vertebrata
Class—Reptilia
Subclass—Diapsida
Superorder—Archosauria
Order—Saurischia
Suborder—Theropoda
Infraorder—Carnosauria
Family—Tyrannosauridae
Genus—Tyrannosaurus
Species—rex

their environment. Dr. Ostrom suggests that some of the dinosaurs, particularly the smaller theropods, might have been true endotherms (warm-blooded animals). He cited the correlation in certain modern animals of high metabolism (the chemical processes in the body that provide energy) and stable body temperatures with erect posture.

Recently, a few paleontologists have expressed their conviction that all dinosaurs were true endotherms: that they sustained high, stable body temperature levels comparable to those of modern mammals and birds. Some of these scientists would like to remove the dinosaurs from Class Reptilia to form their own class. The classification would be:

CLASS DINOSAURIA

Order Saurischia
Order Ornithischia
Order Aves (birds)

Arguments for and against warm-blooded dinosaurs are explored on pages 18 through 21.

Working with Fossils

The fossil record represents hundreds of millions of years of life. As more fossilized remains of prehistoric plants and animals are found, scientists learn new things about the creatures that left them, and theories about their nature change accordingly.

The classification of fossils is a problematical and somewhat arbitrary process. It is not difficult to distinguish a modern reptile from a contemporary mammal or bird, for they represent the results of millions of years of divergent evolution. Classification of modern forms is based on total anatomy, *plus* physiology, behavior, reproduction, and so on—things that are not preserved as fossil evidence. Some fossils are examples of transitional stages between two groups and display characteristics of both, while many others have no modern counterparts. In these cases, a classification must often be made on the basis of very little skeletal information. This is unavoidable and quite necessary, since the classification systems are indispensable to paleontologists. It is not only their job to try to describe an individual species, but to determine its place in the pattern of evolution and determine its relationship to all other animals. By doing so, we can deduce certain information about the individual specimen that might not be clear from the fossil alone, as well as clarify our picture of the history of life on earth.

Unfortunately, when a fossil animal is assigned to a particular class, we tend to attribute to that animal all the characteristics of modern members of it. Since all archosaurs are classified as reptiles because of certain features of their skeletal systems and teeth, we too easily assume that their other systems (circulatory, digestive, nervous, and so on) were reptilian also and that all the "ruling reptiles" behaved like modern lizards, or turtles, or crocodiles.

In the past, dinosaurs have been stereotyped as ponderous, pea-brained hulks barely able to support their own weight. It is true that many of them did have very small brains relative to their enormous bodies, but a number of the smaller dinosaurs had large brain cavities that suggest a high order of intelligence and coordination, perhaps approaching that of modern birds. The fossil record also contains evidence of social behavior among dinosaurs, such as herding and nesting, that we normally associate only with mammals and birds.

The Evolution of Birds

The first known bird, *Archaeopteryx,* appeared about 150 million years ago. Several specimens have been found in the fine limestone deposits near the town of Solnhofen in West Germany. Except for the distinct and detailed impressions of feathers, these fossils are virtually identical to those of small theropods (bipedal carnivores) called coelurosaurs (page 28). Feathers indicate endothermy; they insulate the body, and insulation is counterproductive in ectotherms, because they rely on heat exchange with the environment to maintain a stable body temperature. Only endotherms are insulated.

Paleontologists agree that birds descended from thecodonts, the earliest archosaurs, but the traditional view is that dinosaurs and birds evolved independently from pseudosuchian ancestors, and that any structural similarities were the results of convergent evolution. Convergence is the process by which unrelated or distantly related animals evolve similar structures in response to the demands of similar habitats or life styles; for example, the fins and flippers of dolphins and fish are similar in appearance and function, but the dolphin's flippers evolved out of legs. Dr. Ostrom contends that the similarities between *Archaeopteryx* and the coelurosaurs are too numerous and too striking to attribute to convergence and that birds descended directly from coelurosaurs.

Extinction

At the end of the Mesozoic Era, there was a massive extermination of animal life. An enormous number of life forms perished. This cataclysmic event or series of events apparently occurred some 65 million years ago, changing the face of the earth. We simply don't know what happened. No definitive theory has been proposed that adequately explains why so many animal groups died out, or, more to the point, why the remaining groups survived.

Many theories have been proposed to explain the relatively sudden extinction of the dinosaurs (and pterosaurs). Many people share the misconception that they died out because they were simply unfit. But dinosaurs dominated the land for nearly 140 million years—they were the most successful land vertebrates in the earth's history. In fact, extinction is an inevitable product of the evolutionary processes; it is an ecological phenomenon, the result of critical changes in an organism's relation to its environment.

Finally, we must consider the possibility that the dinosaurs were among the survivors. If birds are indeed the descendants of coelurosaurs, then dinosaurs aren't truly extinct. As Dr. Ostrom says, "Dinosaurs didn't become extinct. They simply flew away."

SYNAPSIDA

Groups of successful, mammal-like reptiles (pelycosaurs and therapsids) prevailed before and during the appearance of the first archosaurs.

Pelycosauria

One of the earliest major groups to evolve from the first reptiles was Order Pelycosauria. The skulls and teeth of these primitive synapsids show mammal-like features. *Dimetrodon* lived about 265 million years ago and grew to a length of 12 feet (3.7 meters). It was the predominant carnivore of its time. Only a few types of pelycosaurs bore the distinctive spinal sails found on *Dimetrodon*. The sails' function is unknown, but they may have been involved in regulating body temperature. *Dimetrodon* might have been closely related to the ancestors of therapsids.

Dimetrodon

Therapsida

Advanced mammal-like reptiles called therapsids evolved later than pelycosaurs and flourished through the Middle Triassic period. They were the dominant land vertebrates throughout most of that time. *Cynognathus* was a large carnivore living during the Early Triassic in southern Africa. Carnivorous therapsids such as *Cynognathus* possessed many of the skeletal and dental characteristics of modern mammals and presumably are their direct ancestors. The first mammals evolved late in the Triassic, and by the end of that period the therapsids were nearly extinct. Only a small group of herbivorous therapsids survived into the Jurassic but then quickly died out.

Skull of *Cynognathus* 15.7 inches (40 cm) long

Cynognathus

Some scientists believe that therapsids such as *Cynognathus* were warm-blooded and covered with fur.

The Evolution of Archosaurs

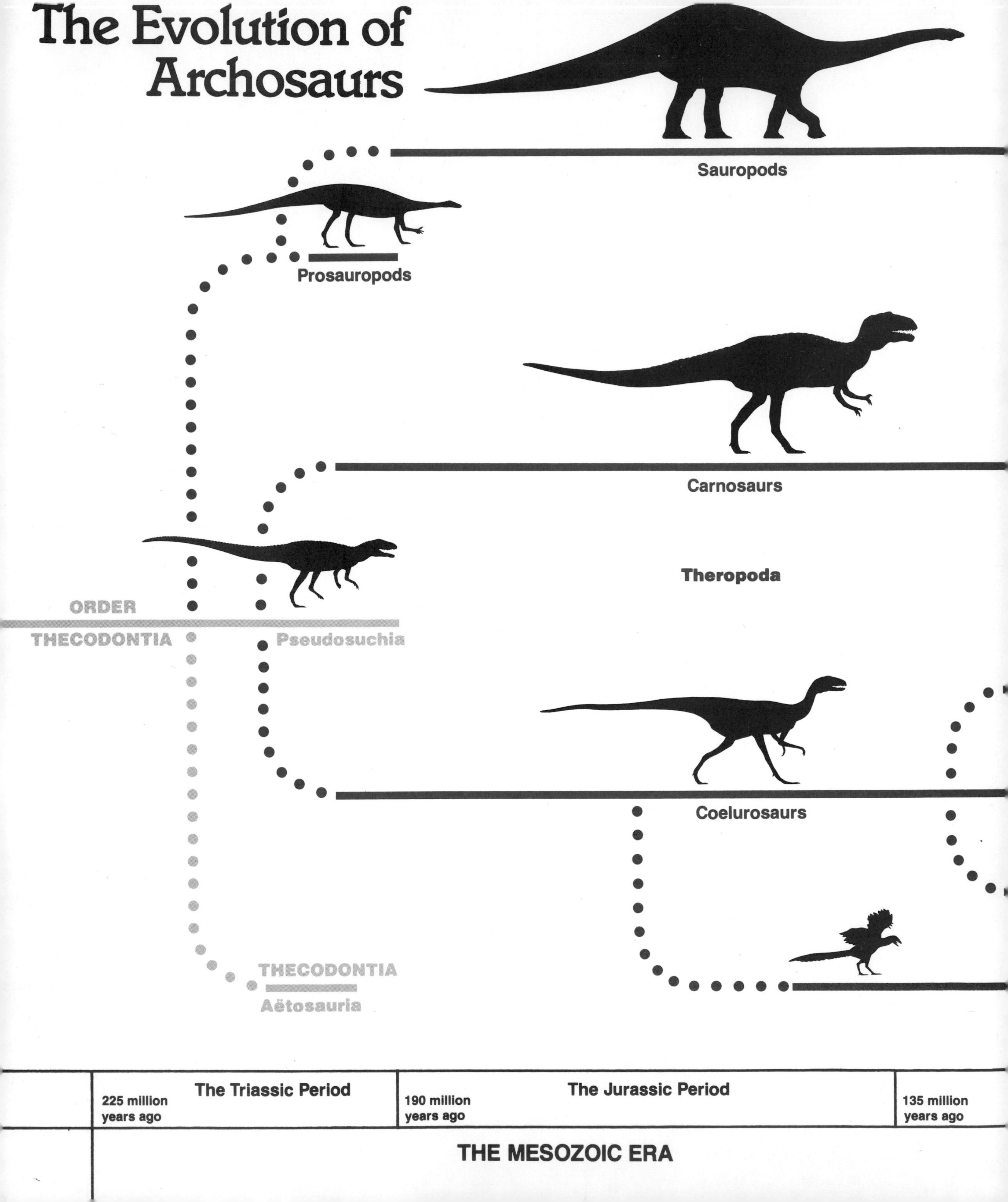

Sauropods

Prosauropods

Carnosaurs

Theropoda

ORDER

THECODONTIA   Pseudosuchia

Coelurosaurs

THECODONTIA

Aëtosauria

	The Triassic Period		The Jurassic Period		
	225 million years ago		190 million years ago		135 million years ago

THE MESOZOIC ERA

Sauropodomorpha

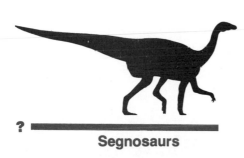

?

Segnosaurs

Order Saurischia

The saurischian order of dinosaurs contains two suborders: Theropoda and Sauropodomorpha. Theropods were bipedal (walked on their hind legs) carnivores, whereas sauropodomorphs were generally quadrupedal (walked on all four legs) herbivores.

SAURISCHIAN HIP

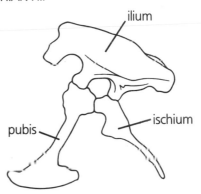

The saurischian hip was usually reptilian in appearance: with the pubis pointing down and forward, and the ischium pointing down and back. There was typically a large angle between these two bones.

Deinocheirosaurs

?

Ornithomimosaurs

Dotted lines represent assumed connections between branches of the archosaurian family tree.

Deinonychosaurs

CLASS

AVES

The Cretaceous Period	65 million years ago	
THE MESOZOIC ERA		**THE CENOZOIC ERA**

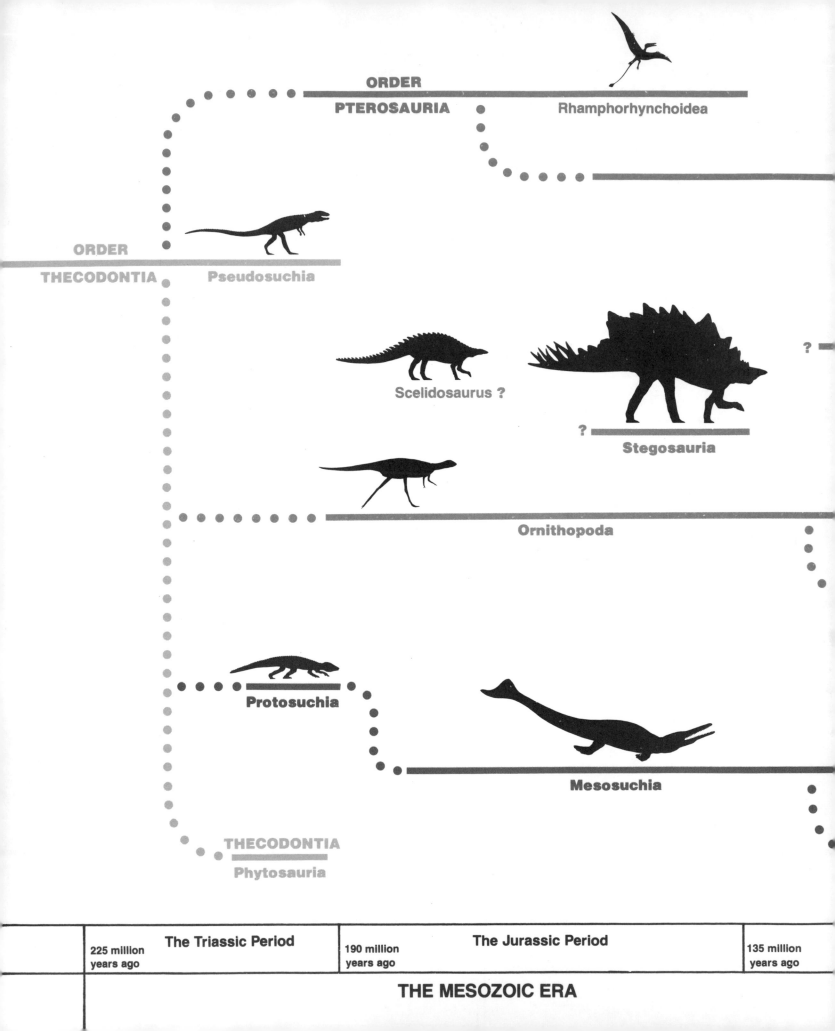

ORDER
PTEROSAURIA   Rhamphorhynchoidea

ORDER
THECODONTIA   Pseudosuchia

Scelidosaurus ?

?

?   Stegosauria

Ornithopoda

Protosuchia

Mesosuchia

THECODONTIA
Phytosauria

	The Triassic Period		The Jurassic Period	
225 million years ago		190 million years ago		135 million years ago

THE MESOZOIC ERA

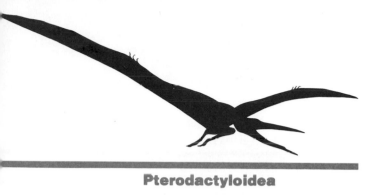

Pterodactyloidea

Order Ornithischia

The ornithischian order contains at least four suborders: Ornithopoda (bipeds), Stegosauria (plated dinosaurs), Ankylosauria (armored dinosaurs), and Ceratopsia (horned dinosaurs).

ORNITHISCHIAN HIP

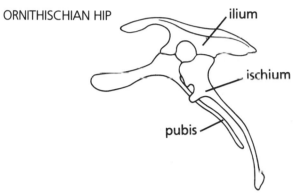

ilium

ischium

pubis

The ornithischian hip was birdlike in appearance, with the pubis directed backward, parallel to the ischium.

Ankylosauria

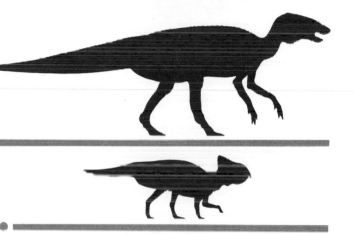

Dotted lines represent assumed connections between branches of the archosaurian family tree.

Ceratopsia

ORDER CROCODILIA

● ?

Eusuchia

The Cretaceous Period	**65 million years ago**	
THE MESOZOIC ERA		**THE CENOZOIC ERA**

Cold-Blooded or Warm-Blooded?

ANIMALS ARE OFTEN described as "cold-blooded" or "warm-blooded." More accurate terms are ectothermic (from the Greek for "outside heat") and endothermic (for "inside heat").

Ectothermic animals receive heat from their environment. To warm up, they move into sunlight. To cool off, they move into shade.

Endothermic animals control the heat inside their bodies. They eat far more food than ectotherms do, converting some of it into heat.

Mammals and birds of today generate their own heat, whereas reptiles are warmed or cooled by the air around them. Dinosaurs, classified as reptiles, have long been considered ectothermic. But some experts now propose that dinosaurs, or at least some of them, were endothermic like birds and mammals. These four pages present arguments for and against this theory.

GEOGRAPHICAL RANGE

Today's archosaurs, the crocodiles, exist only in the tropical and warm temperate zones closest to the equator. But dinosaur fossils have been found on every continent except Antarctica, from the chilly southern tips of Africa, Australia, and South America close to the Arctic Circle. Some paleontologists believe that only endothermic animals could have ranged as far north and south as the dinosaurs did. Others suggest the geographical distribution indicates only that the climate on earth was milder and more uniform than at present. They also point out that the continents have moved from where they were when the dinosaurs lived and died.

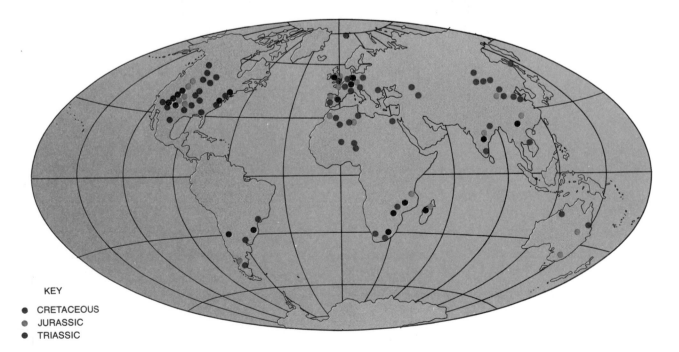

KEY

● CRETACEOUS
● JURASSIC
● TRIASSIC

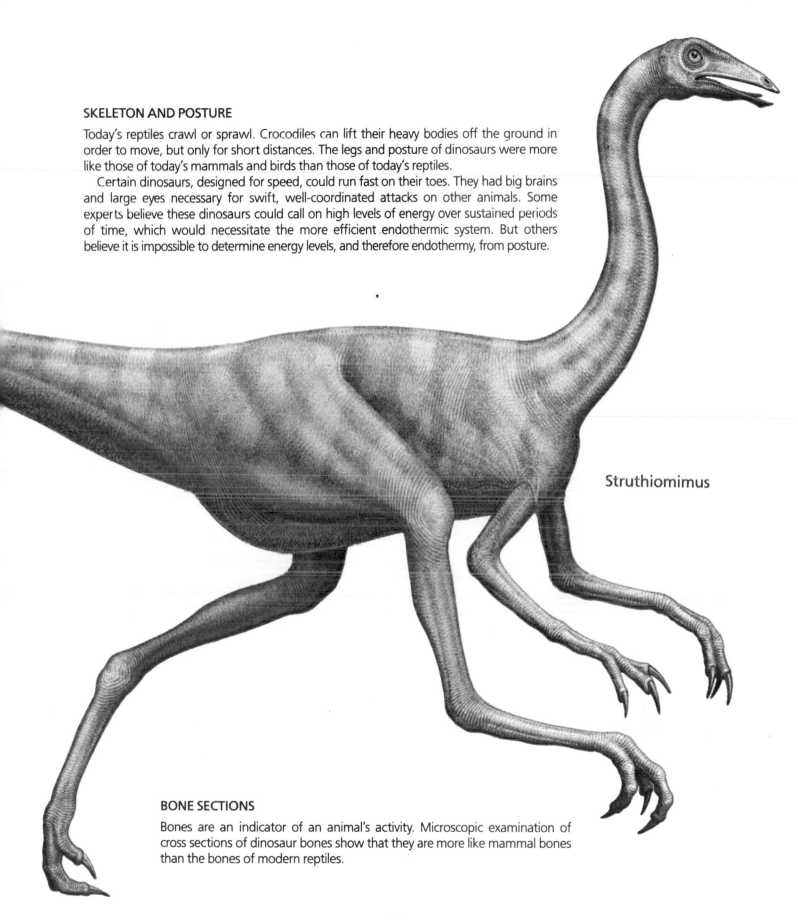

SKELETON AND POSTURE

Today's reptiles crawl or sprawl. Crocodiles can lift their heavy bodies off the ground in order to move, but only for short distances. The legs and posture of dinosaurs were more like those of today's mammals and birds than those of today's reptiles.

Certain dinosaurs, designed for speed, could run fast on their toes. They had big brains and large eyes necessary for swift, well-coordinated attacks on other animals. Some experts believe these dinosaurs could call on high levels of energy over sustained periods of time, which would necessitate the more efficient endothermic system. But others believe it is impossible to determine energy levels, and therefore endothermy, from posture.

Struthiomimus

BONE SECTIONS

Bones are an indicator of an animal's activity. Microscopic examination of cross sections of dinosaur bones show that they are more like mammal bones than the bones of modern reptiles.

FOOD FOR THE LARGEST DINOSAURS

Could a large dinosaur with a small mouth eat enough food to sustain itself? As an endotherm, an adult would need a huge quantity of plant food every day.

If the giant dinosaurs were ectothermic, however, they would need to eat a fraction of that amount. At a time when the climate was mild and stable, without cold winters, their massive bodies would act as reservoirs of heat. This way, a large dinosaur could maintain a stable temperature without being endothermic.

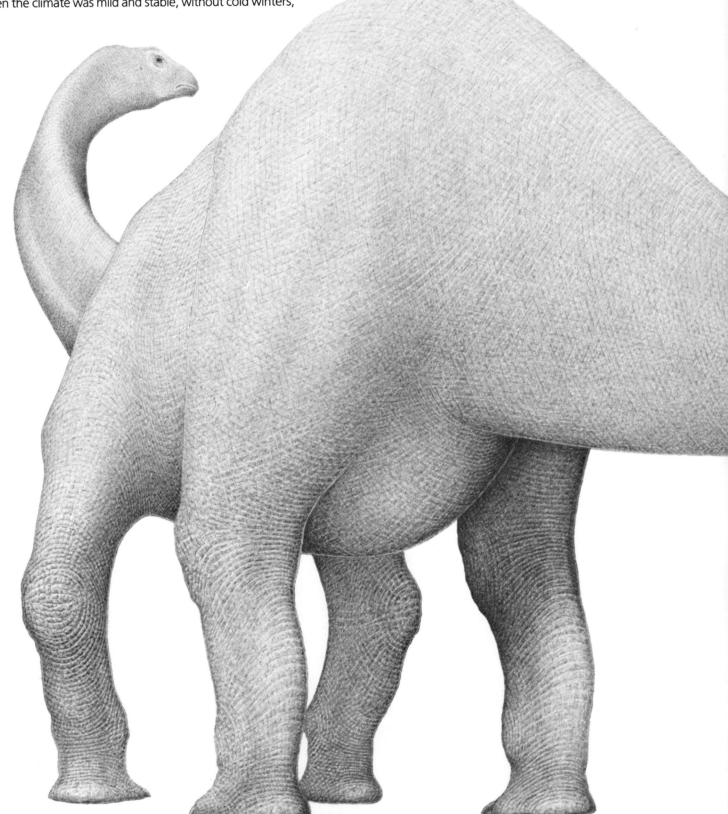

PREDATORS AND PREY

An endotherm needs much more food than an ectotherm of the same size. A community of endothermic predators requires a larger prey population than does a community of ectothermic predators. Dinosaur predator-prey ratios are much closer to those of mammals than to those of reptiles.

This argument depends on the assumption that the fossil record reflects the true relative abundance of dinosaur groups in the Mesozoic communities. Most scientists are not willing to accept this assumption. Moreover, even if these statistics were valid, they only concern predators. The prey population could just as well have been ectothermic.

CHAMBERS OF THE HEART

All modern mammals and birds have efficient hearts with four separate chambers, two of which pump blood to the lungs at a lower pressure than to the rest of the body. But modern reptiles have less efficient hearts (one pump chamber) which pump blood to their lungs and hearts at the same pressure.

If the heart of *Ultrasaurus* (pages 46–47) had to pump blood to its lungs at the same pressure as to its head, 60 feet (18.6 meters) high, its lungs would have filled with fluid. *Ultrasaurus* would have drowned. So the erect posture of dinosaurs suggests that they had the more efficient hearts—like the mammals and birds of today.

FEATHERS FOR INSULATION

Today's small endothermic animals, including birds, need a special body layer to insulate their bodies. *Archaeopteryx*, which had feathers, is the earliest known bird. Its skeleton is almost identical to that of certain small dinosaurs, and it seems that *Archaeopteryx* was just a short evolutionary step from its dinosaurian ancestors.

Other experts believe *Archaeopteryx* was not closely related to dinosaurs, pointing out that there is no direct evidence of insulation in dinosaurs themselves.

THE DOMINANT DINOSAURS

The first dinosaurs and the first mammals appeared at about the same time. Endothermy is generally considered advantageous because a "warm-blooded" animal can be continuously more active than an ectotherm. Therefore the dinosaurs that dominated the presumably endothermic mammals for 140 million years should have been endothermic too. But some scientists feel that dinosaurs might have been dominant only because they reached large sizes before the mammals did.

21

Triassic Period

THE TRIASSIC, the first period of the Mesozoic Era, lasted for about 35 million years—from 225 million to 190 million years ago. *Triassic* comes from *trias*, the Latin word for "three," named for three rock layers formed during this period.

At the beginning of the Triassic, the continents made up a single land mass known as Pangaea (see the map on the next page). Because there were no substantial seas, mountains, or temperature barriers, animals could migrate freely from one area of Pangaea to another.

The climate was rather dry during the Triassic and apparently grew warmer throughout the period. The warming climate fostered the expansion of plant and animal life on land.

During this period land vertebrates (animals with backbones) changed enormously. In fact, all the major tetrapod (four-legged-animal) groups were replaced in the Triassic. All the tetrapods that dominated the Mesozoic Era—as well as those that populate our world today—first appeared in significant numbers during the Triassic. These comprise frogs, lizards, turtles, marine reptiles, archosaurs (including the ancestors of birds), and mammals.

Although a few varieties of the mammal-like therapsids (page 13) survived into the Jurassic, by the end of the Triassic they were virtually extinct. Moreover, the thecodonts (pages 26–27) had been replaced by dinosaurs and crocodiles, and the first pterosaurs were in the air.

This montage of Triassic plants and animals includes reconstructions of *Plateosaurus,* a prosauropod (page 30); *Megazostrodon,* a primitive mammal; *Procompsognathus,* a coelurosaur (page 28); and the pterosaur *Eudimorphodon* (page 32) as they might have appeared in life. *Araucarioxylon* and the broad-leafed *Palaeocycas* are typical plants of the period. *Equisetum* is identical to living horsetails.

The fossils are the remains of a pair of *Coelophysis* (page 28); the fern *Phlebopteris; Clionites,* a tentacled mollusk related to the chambered nautilus; *Thrinaxodon,* an advanced early Triassic therapsid; and a track of coelurosaur footprints.

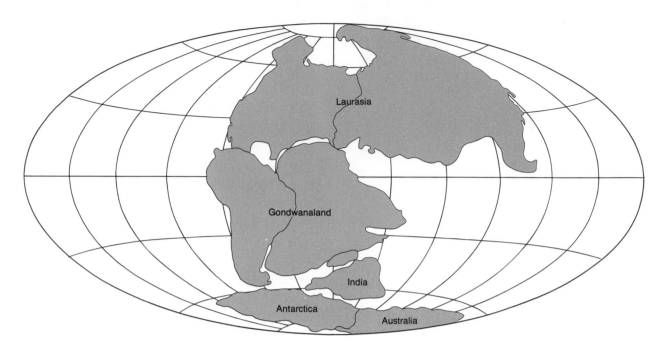

The world as it was about 180–200 million years ago in Late Triassic time, as the supercontinent Pangaea began to break apart.

The first great order of dinosaurs, Order Saurischia, comprises two suborders: Theropoda and Sauropodomorpha.

Theropods

The theropods were meat eaters. They walked on their hind legs, with tails outstretched to counterbalance their bodies.

Late in the Triassic period, small, agile theropods called coelurosaurs (page 28) evolved from thecodonts. The coelurosaurs persisted throughout the Mesozoic, some families differing little from Triassic coelurosaurs, others evolving into a variety of forms.

A second group of theropods appears somewhat later in the Triassic record. Carnosaurs (page 29) were big beasts with more solid, heavy bones. They had large, deep skulls supported by short, muscular necks, and their forelimbs were proportionately shorter than those of the coelurosaurs.

Sauropodomorphs

The earliest sauropodomorphs are classified in the infraorder Prosauropoda.

Prosauropods lived and died out during the Late Triassic. They had small skulls attached to fairly long necks. The fossil record indicates that they grew progressively larger and increasingly quadrupedal.

In the past, prosauropods were considered to be ancestors of the huge Jurassic and Cretaceous sauropods (pages 44–47)—a transitional stage that led to "brontosaurs." Some scientists now doubt that prosauropods were ancestors of the sauropods. These scientists believe that prosauropods were a separate line that simply died out.

Ornithischians

Fossils of Triassic ornithischians are fragmentary and in most cases there seems to be considerable doubt that they should be assigned to this period.

Pterosaurs

The first true flying vertebrates were the Late Triassic pterosaurs. The arms of the pterosaurs were similar to those of other tetrapods, but they had greatly elongated fourth fingers. Each forelimb supported a reinforced wing membrane extending from the tip of the fourth finger to the side of the trunk. The first three fingers were typically reptilian and bore sharp claws; the fifth finger was absent.

Order Pterosauria comprises the suborders Rhamphorhynchoidea and Pterodactyloidea. Pterodactyloids apparently evolved from rhamphorhynchoids. All known Triassic pterosaurs are rhamphorhynchoids.

For over a century scientists have speculated that pterosaurs must have been warm-blooded, because flying requires sustained high energy levels. In 1971, this hypothesis appears to have been confirmed. A little fossil rhamphorhynchoid, found in the Soviet Union, showed that the animal was covered with hair.

Crocodiles

Order Crocodilia contains three suborders: Protosuchia, Mesosuchia, and Eusuchia. The classification of a particular genus depends primarily on two features: the location of the internal nares (the openings of the nasal passage that admit air through the windpipe into the lungs) and the shape of the vertebrae.

Modern crocodiles belong to the suborder Eusuchia. They have a substantial secondary palate (roof of the mouth) that separates the nasal and oral cavities. The internal nares are toward the rear of the skull near the throat. In protosuchians, the most primitive crocodiles, these openings are near the nostrils.

The vertebrae of eusuchians are concave (arch inward) in front and convex (bulge outward) in back, resulting in a ball-and-socket joint. Protosuchians have vertebrae that are concave on both ends.

All crocodilian specimens from the Triassic period are protosuchians.

THECODONTIA

The first thecodonts belong to the suborder Proterosuchia. Thecodonts were quite rare in the Early Triassic period, when therapsids (mammal-like reptiles) were the dominant life forms. However, by the middle of the Triassic, thecodonts had become dominant. Three new suborders of thecodonts had evolved: pseudosuchians, phytosaurs, and aëtosaurs. Pseudosuchians included the apparent ancestors of all later archosaurs.

Thecodonts stood more erect than the sprawling reptiles from which they evolved. It was probably this improved posture that gave them an advantage over therapsids. As thecodonts began to move about on their long hind legs, their shorter front limbs became free for other things such as balance, grasping, and so on. Many pseudosuchians could apparently run on their hind legs.

Desmatosuchus was an aëtosaur of the Late Triassic in Texas. Aëtosaurs were heavily armored and lived on land.

Chasmatosaurus was a primitive proterosuchian of the Early Triassic in South Africa, China, India, and Russia.

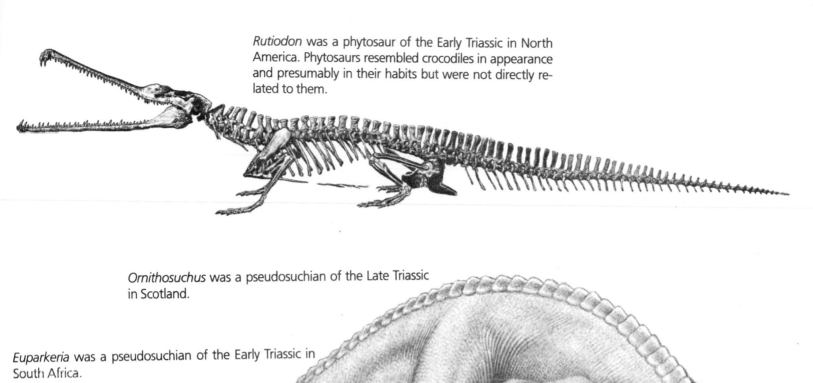

Rutiodon was a phytosaur of the Early Triassic in North America. Phytosaurs resembled crocodiles in appearance and presumably in their habits but were not directly related to them.

Ornithosuchus was a pseudosuchian of the Late Triassic in Scotland.

Euparkeria was a pseudosuchian of the Early Triassic in South Africa.

Euparkeria

THEROPODA

Coelurosaurs

Among the earliest dinosaurs were theropods called coelurosaurs. In the Triassic period they were relatively small, active meat eaters. They had long, delicate limb bones, many of them hollow. Coelurosaurs had shallow, narrow skulls with sharp, knifelike teeth lining their jaws. They always walked on their hind legs and had long, slender necks, grasping fingers, and birdlike feet.

Using their long tails to balance their bodies, coelurosaurs ran on their toes. They were obviously built for speed. *Procompsognathus* and *Coelophysis* were typical coelurosaurs of the Late Triassic.

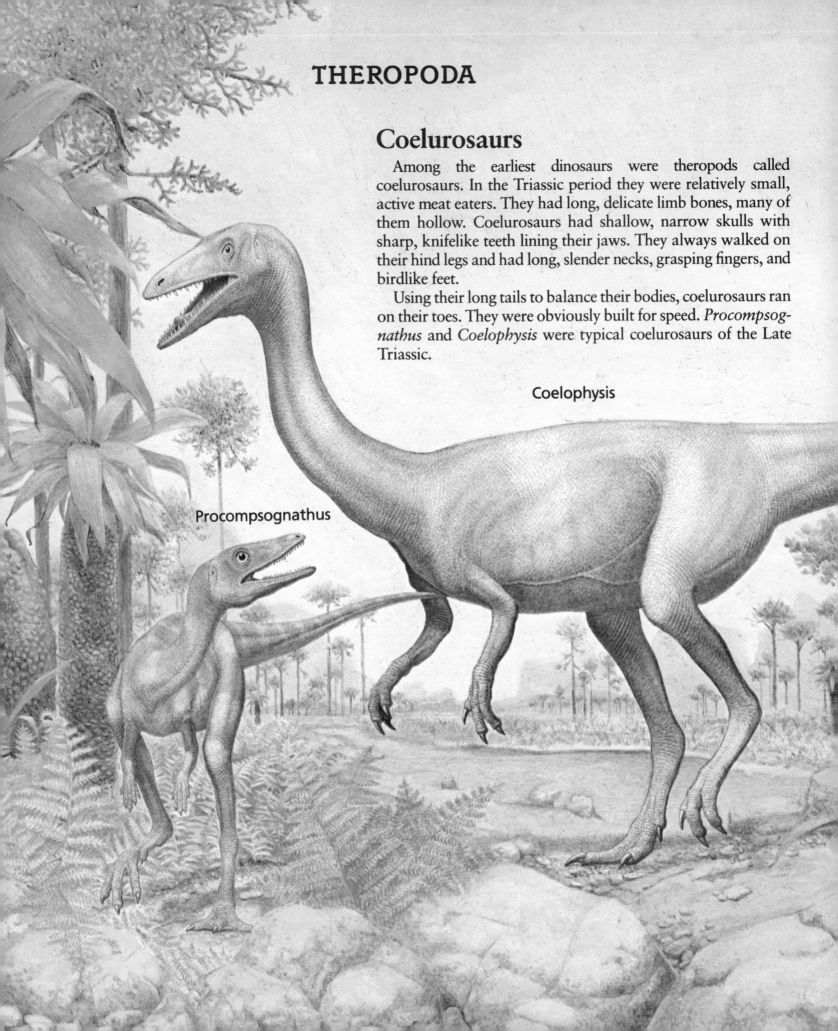

Coelophysis

Procompsognathus

Carnosaurs

Carnosaurs such as *Teratosaurus* apparently evolved somewhat later than the coelurosaurs. Like coelurosaurs, carnosaurs walked on their hind legs, but they were larger and more robust. Their hind legs were proportionally shorter than those of the swift little coelurosaurs, and their bones were heavy and often solid. Carnosaurs had short, muscular necks supporting large, deep skulls. Their jaws were armed with daggerlike teeth with serrated edges.

Teratosaurus

SAUROPODOMORPHA

Prosauropods

The prosauropods are generally classified in three major families. Prosauropods were probably herbivorous.

Plateosaurus

Anchisaurus

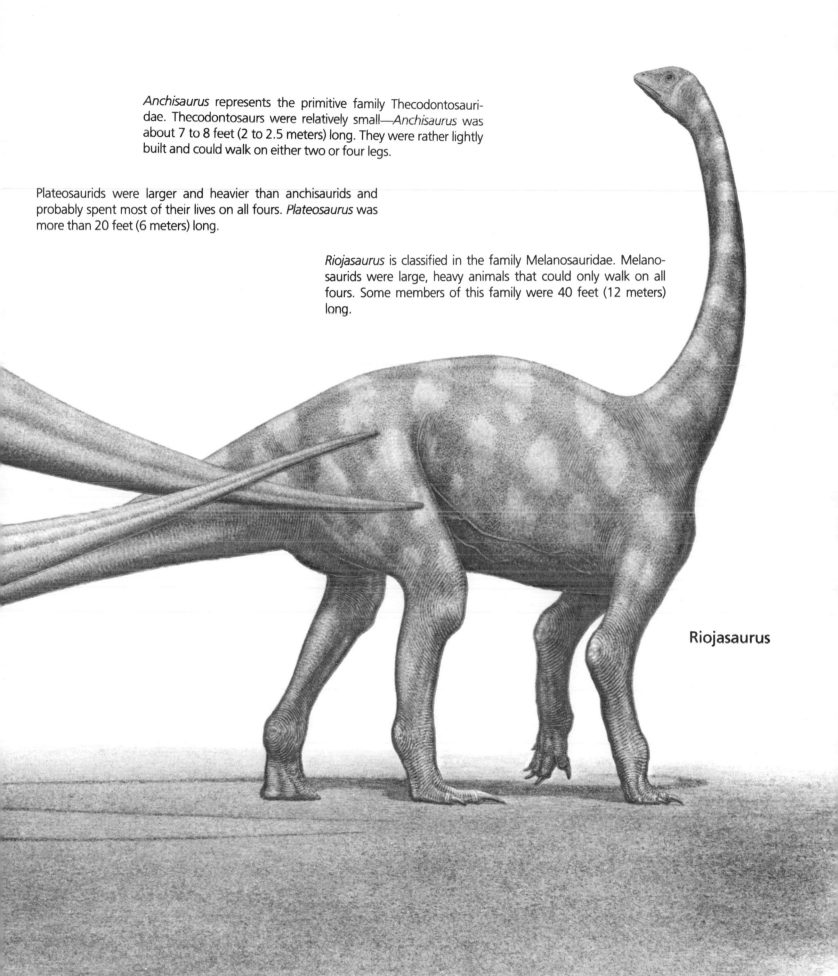

Anchisaurus represents the primitive family Thecodontosauridae. Thecodontosaurs were relatively small—*Anchisaurus* was about 7 to 8 feet (2 to 2.5 meters) long. They were rather lightly built and could walk on either two or four legs.

Plateosaurids were larger and heavier than anchisaurids and probably spent most of their lives on all fours. *Plateosaurus* was more than 20 feet (6 meters) long.

Riojasaurus is classified in the family Melanosauridae. Melanosaurids were large, heavy animals that could only walk on all fours. Some members of this family were 40 feet (12 meters) long.

Riojasaurus

PTEROSAURIA

Rhamphorhynchoidea

The Triassic pterosaurs belong to the suborder Rhamphorhynchoidea. Robust, powerful fliers, rhamphorhynchoids had large heads on relatively long necks and a heavy dental battery. *Eudimorphodon*, which lived in northern Italy during the Late Triassic, displayed a varied array of teeth. Some were the simple spikes associated with modern reptiles, but others were more complex, having several cusps.

Eudimorphodon was about 20 inches (50 cm) long with a 35-to-40-inch (87-to-100-cm) wingspan.

Rhamphorhynchoids had short metacarpals (the bones between the wrists and fingers), long fourth fingers, and a strangely shaped fifth toe, the function of which is unknown. They also had long reptilian tails.

Eudimorphodon

CROCODILIA

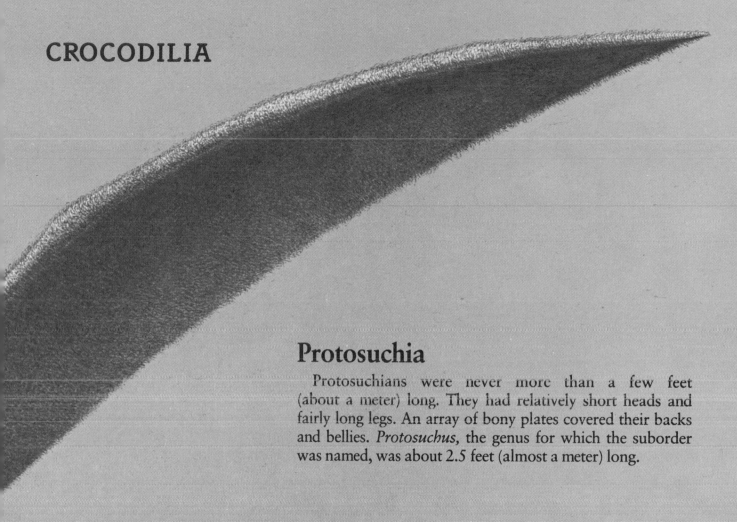

Protosuchia

Protosuchians were never more than a few feet (about a meter) long. They had relatively short heads and fairly long legs. An array of bony plates covered their backs and bellies. *Protosuchus*, the genus for which the suborder was named, was about 2.5 feet (almost a meter) long.

Protosuchus

Jurassic Period

THE MIDDLE PERIOD of the Mesozoic Era, the Jurassic, lasted for about 55 million years—from 190 million to 135 million years ago. The period is named for the Jura Mountains in the Alps, on the border between France and Switzerland, where many rock layers dating from that period have been discovered.

Pangaea (see the map on page 24) was breaking into two supercontinents—Laurasia in the north and Gondwanaland in the south—with the Tethys Sea opening up between them. But there were still connections between the two land masses, and animals spread freely across them.

The warming trend of the Late Triassic continued into the Jurassic period. Shallow seas invaded portions of Laurasia, and abundant rainfall reached areas that had previously been arid and desertlike. The climate became moist and mild. Plant life flourished in swamps, beside lakes and rivers, and across broad plains.

Similar plants have been found across the globe. Fossils of semitropical plants have been found as far north as Siberia and Alaska and as far south as Antarctica. With the development of these vast new food supplies, a great variety of plant-eating dinosaurs evolved. They provided an ample and varied food supply for larger and larger meat-eating dinosaurs.

This Late Jurassic landscape is a composite of reconstructions from two areas of the world. The small animals in the foreground are all from limestone deposits in Germany: *Archaeopteryx,* the oldest known bird (pages 40–41); *Compsognathus,* a coelurosaur (page 39); and *Rhamphorhynchus,* a pterosaur (page 54).

Behind them are large dinosaurs from Wyoming and Colorado. As *Stegosaurus* (pages 52–53) looks on, a pair of *Allosaurus* (pages 42–43) stalk a *Camptosaurus* (page 50).

Plants include *Williamsonia* and the squat *Cycadeoidea,* a field of ferns, and a forest of evergreens.

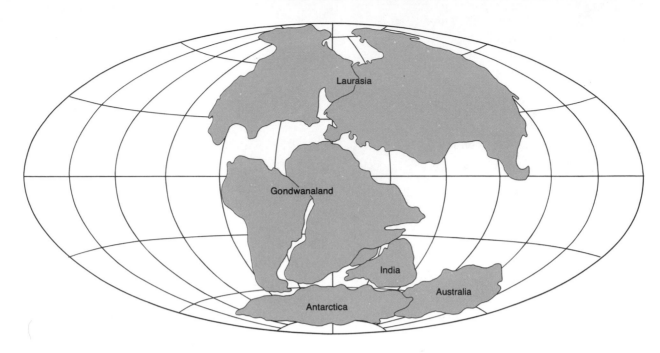

By Late Jurassic time, 140 million years ago, the North Atlantic Ocean had formed and a rift had developed between South America and southern Africa.

Theropods and the First Bird

Jurassic theropods were not structurally very different from their Triassic ancestors. But they varied more in size as the dinosaur community expanded to fill a broad range of ecological niches. Some coelurosaurs were no larger than chickens, whereas some of the carnosaurs grew up to 40 feet (12 meters) long.

The first known bird dates from the Late Jurassic. Its fossil skeletons are remarkably similar to those of small meat-eating theropods.

Sauropodomorphs

During the Jurassic great herds of sauropods replaced the prosauropods of the Triassic (pages 30–31). Sauropods (pages 44–47) included the largest animals ever known, some possibly weighing up to 100 tons (90.7 metric tons). They were all herbivores and always walked on four feet.

Most paleontologists once believed that the large brontosaurs were too heavy to support themselves on dry land and had to spend most of their lives in the water. These scientists assumed that the buoyancy of the water compensated for the animals' extraordinary weight. Recent analysis of the skeletal structure of sauropods, however, indicates that they were perfectly capable of living on land and were in fact much better adapted for terrestrial life. Fossil tracks also show that some sauropods did walk on land.

The heads of the sauropods were very small in relation to their large bodies. It is difficult to understand how they could eat enough to survive. Moreover, their teeth were often rather simple pegs only at the front of their mouths. They had no grinding teeth. However, smoothly polished stones have been found with the fossils of some specimens. It seems that these plant eaters, including the sauropods, swallowed stones to grind up food in their gizzards—as modern birds and crocodiles do. If so, the sauropods could have eaten almost continuously, swallowing their food unchewed.

Ornithischians

Most of the known Triassic dinosaurs belong to the saurischian order. But during the Jurassic period, the second order of dinosaurs, the ornithischians, rose and flourished. All known Jurassic ornithischians were herbivorous.

There were at least two Jurassic suborders of Order Ornithischia; Ornithopoda and Stegosauria. Ornithopods were bipeds.

When the small ornithopods *Lesothosaurus* and *Heterodontosaurus* (page 48) were discovered in southern Africa, they were thought to be Triassic in origin. Now many paleontologists ascribe the rock beds in which they were found to the Early Jurassic, so they will be considered in this chapter.

Hypsilophodonts (page 49) were small, lightly built, rather primitive ornithopods with long legs.

Iguanodonts were more heavily built ornithopods, known from the Late Jurassic and Early Cretaceous, and grew to more than 25 feet (7.8 meters) in length. *Iguanodon* was one of Owen's original Dinosauria. The primitive Jurassic iguanodonts were called camptosaurs.

Stegosauria included some of the most bizarre-looking of all the dinosaurs, with rows of plates and spikes along their backs. They walked on four feet.

Until the discovery of *Heterodontosaurus* in 1962, *Scelidosaurus* was the oldest known ornithischian. *Scelidosaurus*' relationships to other ornithischians are uncertain.

Pterosaurs

Although they were only distantly related to flying birds through early archosaurian ancestors, pterosaurs evolved a number of similarities to them. These were responses to the requirements of flight, the result of convergent evolution. Weight reduction was achieved through a fragile skeletal structure of hollow bones and a progressive tendency to lighten and finally eliminate reptilian teeth. Parts of the skeleton were fused along lines of maximum stress. A keeled breastbone anchored strong flight muscles. The areas of the brain responsible for coordination and vision were much enlarged.

Crocodiles

Crocodiles of the suborder Mesosuchia were abundant throughout the Jurassic. The mesosuchians ranged in size from less than a foot to around 20 feet (30 cm to 6 meters) long. Like the protosuchians, their vertebrae were concave on both ends, but their internal nares were farther back in their skulls. Most mesosuchians were active hunters and prowled lowland swamps and shores much like their modern archosaurian relatives—today's crocodiles, alligators, and gavials. But some returned to the sea.

Ornitholestes

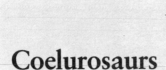

Coelurosaurs

The Jurassic coelurosaurs were similar in many respects to their Triassic ancestors. *Ornitholestes* was typical. It was about 6 feet (2 meters) in length, with long legs and birdlike feet. Its arms were somewhat shorter than its legs, and each hand had three long fingers armed with sharp claws.

Compsognathus is the smallest known coelurosaur, only about 2 feet (60 cm) long. The first specimen was found in the limestone deposits near Solnhofen, West Germany.

Some paleontologists believe that *Compsognathus* was warm-blooded and feathered. However, there is no direct evidence to support this hypothesis.

Compsognathus

CLASS AVES

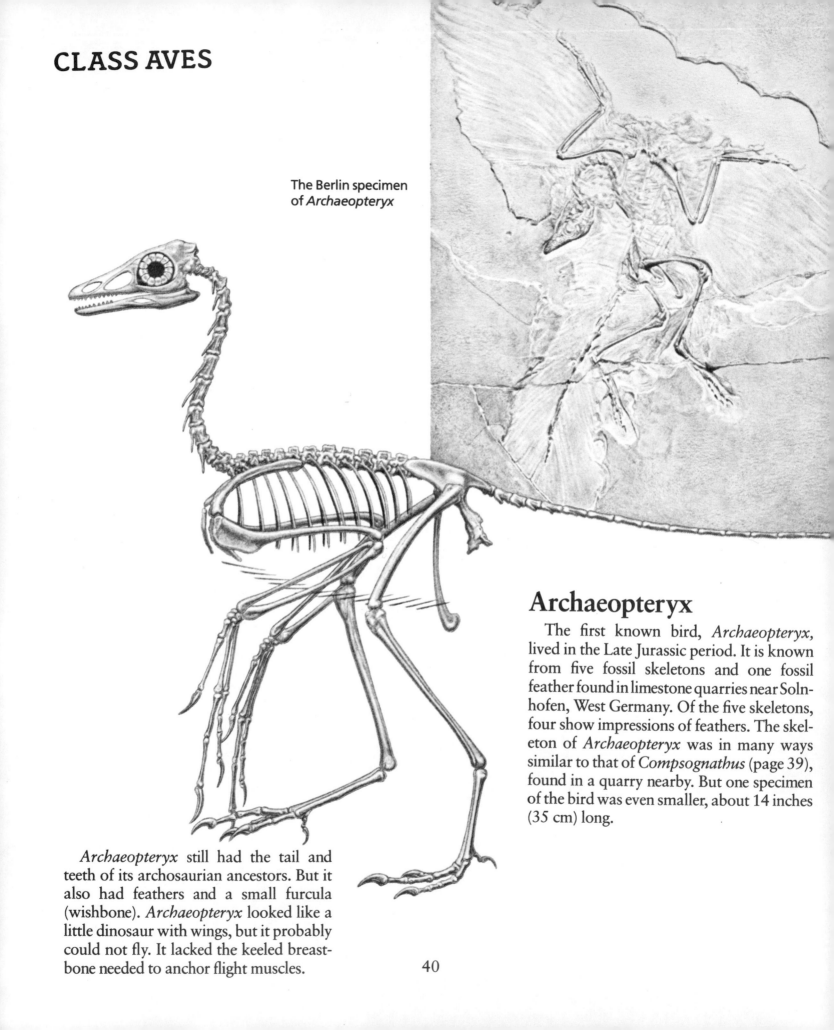

The Berlin specimen
of *Archaeopteryx*

Archaeopteryx

The first known bird, *Archaeopteryx,* lived in the Late Jurassic period. It is known from five fossil skeletons and one fossil feather found in limestone quarries near Solnhofen, West Germany. Of the five skeletons, four show impressions of feathers. The skeleton of *Archaeopteryx* was in many ways similar to that of *Compsognathus* (page 39), found in a quarry nearby. But one specimen of the bird was even smaller, about 14 inches (35 cm) long.

Archaeopteryx still had the tail and teeth of its archosaurian ancestors. But it also had feathers and a small furcula (wishbone). *Archaeopteryx* looked like a little dinosaur with wings, but it probably could not fly. It lacked the keeled breastbone needed to anchor flight muscles.

40

Two theories explain the evolution of flight in birds. The first is that the ancestors of *Archaeopteryx* were tree climbers and that it evolved as a glider. However, the foot of *Archaeopteryx* doesn't seem to be suitable for living in trees. The first toe is too short and placed too high to be effective in perching.

The second theory is that *Archaeopteryx* developed as a running insectivore (insect eater). Feathers first evolved for insulation. The lengthening of forelimb and tail feathers and of the bones of the arms and hands may have been directly involved with the pursuit of insects. *Archaeopteryx* was preadapted for flight.

Archaeopteryx

THEROPODA

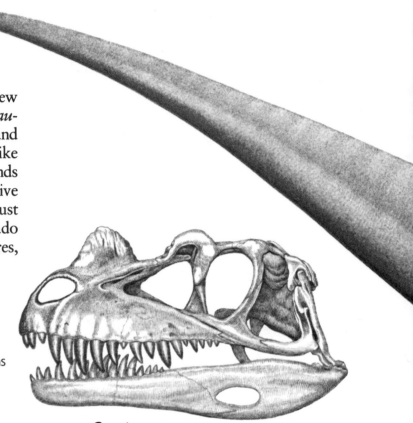

Carnosaurs

During the Jurassic period some meat eaters grew far larger than their relatives of the Triassic. *Allosaurus* measured up to 40 feet (12 meters) in length and weighed perhaps up to 6 tons (5.4 metric tons). Like the earlier carnosaurs, it had sharp claws on its hands and long talons on its feet, undoubtedly very effective as weapons. This beautifully designed predator must have been the scourge of Jurassic lands of Colorado and Wyoming as it preyed on a variety of herbivores, including the giant *Apatosaurus*.

Ceratosaurus, a contemporary of *Allosaurus*, was about the same size.

Ceratosaurus

Allosaurus

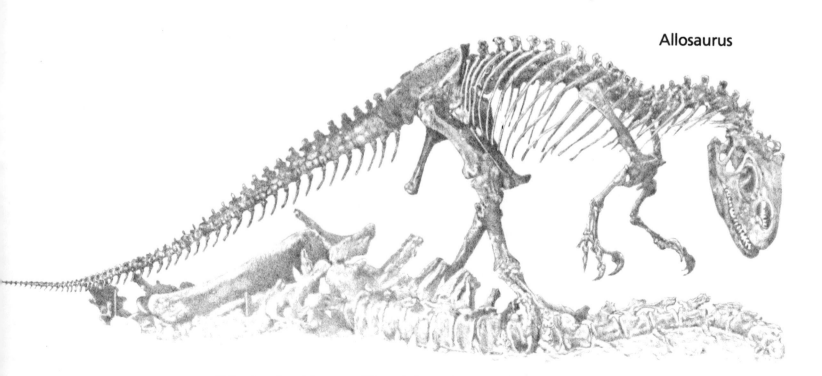

At the American Museum of Natural History in New York City, a skeleton of *Allosaurus* was mounted above a skeleton of *Apatosaurus*. Teeth marks were found in the tailbones of the *Apatosaurus* specimen which matched the spacing of *Allosaurus* teeth.

Allosaurus

SAUROPODOMORPHA

Sauropods

Sauropods included the largest beasts that have ever walked the earth. Although they have been found throughout the Jurassic and Cretaceous periods, the largest examples and the densest populations are from the Late Jurassic.

Four strong, solid legs supported the enormous trunk, long neck, and surprisingly small head. The nostrils of some sauropods were high on their heads rather than on their snouts. The tail was thick and muscular at the base but slender and whiplike at the end.

The jaws and teeth of the sauropods were rather simple, perhaps suitable only for eating soft plant material. These giants may have munched on the leaves of trees too high for other animals to reach. A large sauropod needed to eat about 500 to 1,000 pounds (230 to 450 kilograms) of plant food each day.

Apatosaurus, popularly known as *Brontosaurus*, has been found in the Rocky Mountain area and in Europe. The largest were about 75 feet (23 meters) long and weighed 20 tons (18 metric tons) or more. Fossilized tracks show that these sauropods sometimes traveled in herds. No dragging-tail marks have been found with the footprints, so brontosaurs apparently walked with their tails held above the ground. To protect the younger animals from meat-eating dinosaurs such as *Allosaurus*, the largest adults appear to have traveled on the outside of the herd.

Apatosaurus (Brontosaurus)

SAUROPODOMORPHA

Sauropods

Until recently the largest known land animal was the sauropod *Brachiosaurus*. A *Brachiosaurus* mounted in the East Berlin Museum is 70 feet (22 meters) long and might have weighed close to 80 tons (72.6 metric tons)—more than 10 large elephants. Its front legs, unlike those of most other sauropods, were longer than its hind legs. The high shoulders and long neck placed the animal's head 40 feet (12 meters) above the ground.

In 1972 a massive shoulderblade, 8 feet (2.5 meters) long, was unearthed at Dry Mesa Quarry in Colorado. A vertebra probably from the same animal is 5 feet (1.6 meters) long. The shoulderblade and the vertebra belonged to a dinosaur nicknamed "Supersaurus." If it was a species of *Brachiosaurus*, it would have been almost 50 feet (16 meters) tall.

In 1979 parts of an animal with a shoulderblade 9 feet (2.8 meters) long were discovered at Dry Mesa Quarry. If this "Ultrasaurus" was a species of *Brachiosaurus*, it might have stood nearly 60 feet (19 meters) tall.

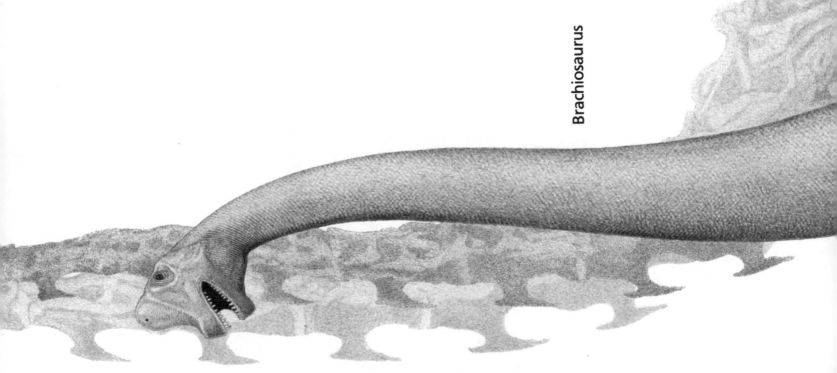

Brachiosaurus

Ultrasaurus

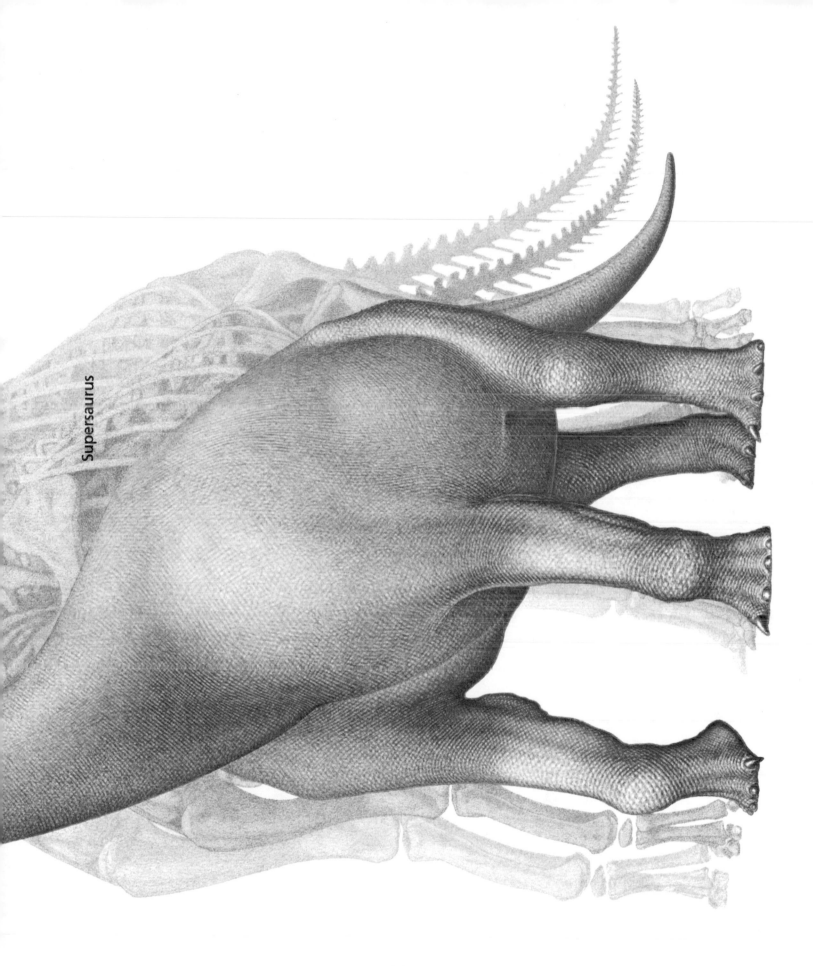

Supersaurus

ORNITHOPODA

Two small and primitive ornithopods were found in the 1960s in southern Africa: *Lesothosaurus* in Lesotho (Basutoland) and *Heterodontosaurus* in the Cape province. Both were about 3 feet (1 meter) long.

Heterodontosaurus had three kinds of teeth, variety not usually found in reptiles. In the front of its upper jaw were small, simple teeth that bit against the predentary. In the back of the jaws were tall teeth, honed to form scissorlike cutting edges.

The most striking of the teeth were the "canine" fangs, between the nipping and slicing teeth of the upper jaw and just behind the predentary of the lower jaw. Like later ornithischians, *Heterodontosaurus* had muscular cheeks to contain its food as it chewed.

Lesothosaurus is considered to be an archetypical early ornithopod, resembling the ancestors from which all ornithopods (and perhaps all ornithischians) evolved. In many ways, it is the most primitive known ornithischian. *Lesothosaurus* apparently lacked the muscular cheeks associated with most ornithischians, and its teeth were unspecialized.

Heterodontosaurus

Lesothosaurus

Hypsilophodonts were small, agile ornithopods that retained many of the primitive features of their ancestors. Their legs were quite long, and because their foot bones (metatarsals) were proportionally longer than those of other ornithopods, they were probably faster. *Dryosaurus* was a large, Late Jurassic hypsilophodont. It grew to lengths of 10 to 12 feet (3 to 3.7 meters).

Dryosaurus

Camptosaurs, found in Europe and North America, were the earliest and least specialized of the iguanodonts. To flee from *Allosaurus* or other meat eaters, *Camptosaurus* could run on its hind legs. But its stocky arms and broad hands suggest that it stood on all fours to feed. Various species of *Camptosaurus* ranged from 4 to 15 feet (1.2 to 4.7 meters) in length.

Surviving from the Middle Jurassic to the Early Cretaceous period, iguanodonts may have been the ancestors of the hadrosaurs (pages 70–71).

Camptosaurus

Few examples of *Scelidosaurus* have been found, all in southern England and dating from the Early Jurassic period. The skeleton is that of a heavily built animal, about 12 feet (3.7 meters) long. With its small head and rather weak jaws, it probably browsed among soft plants. Possibly for protection from large meat-eating dinosaurs, it had solid bony plates set in the skin of its back.

Scelidosaurus has been considered to be an early stegosaur or an ancestor of the ankylosaurs (pages 74–75). Perhaps it was neither.

Scelidosaurus

STEGOSAURIA

Stegosaurus

The best known of the plated dinosaurs is *Stegosaurus*, found in Jurassic deposits of Colorado and Wyoming. Its most distinctive feature was a double row of large, bony plates set alternately in the skin along the neck, back, and tail. Some paleontologists used to think that these plates lay flat against the body, perhaps as protection against large meat eaters such as *Allosaurus*. Now experts believe that the plates stood upright and contained networks of blood vessels. If so, the plates might have served as heat exchangers to regulate body temperature.

Stegosaurus ranged up to 18 feet (5.6 meters) in length and weighed about 2 to 3 tons (1.8 to 2.7 metric tons). But its head was no larger than that of a big dog, and its brain was quite small. Its hind legs were much longer than its front legs, in some species more than twice as long. But *Stegosaurus* probably stood and walked on all four feet. *Stegosaurus* may have swung its spiked tail as a defensive weapon against meat-eating dinosaurs.

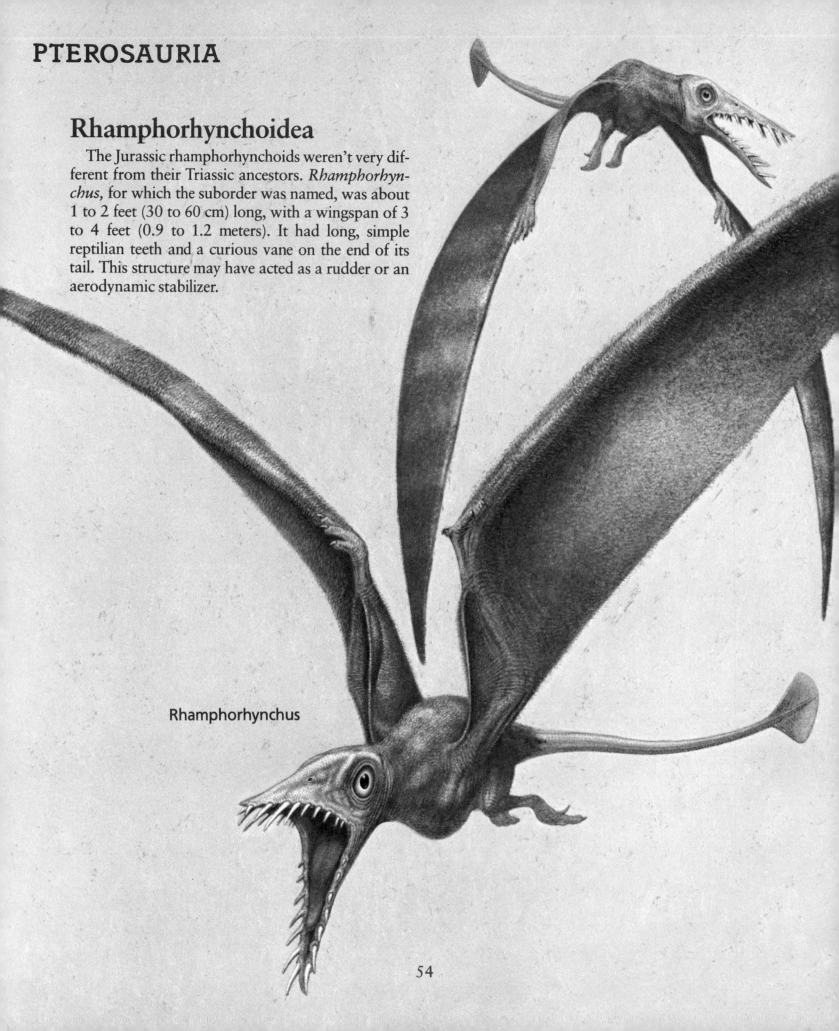

PTEROSAURIA

Rhamphorhynchoidea

The Jurassic rhamphorhynchoids weren't very different from their Triassic ancestors. *Rhamphorhynchus,* for which the suborder was named, was about 1 to 2 feet (30 to 60 cm) long, with a wingspan of 3 to 4 feet (0.9 to 1.2 meters). It had long, simple reptilian teeth and a curious vane on the end of its tail. This structure may have acted as a rudder or an aerodynamic stabilizer.

Rhamphorhynchus

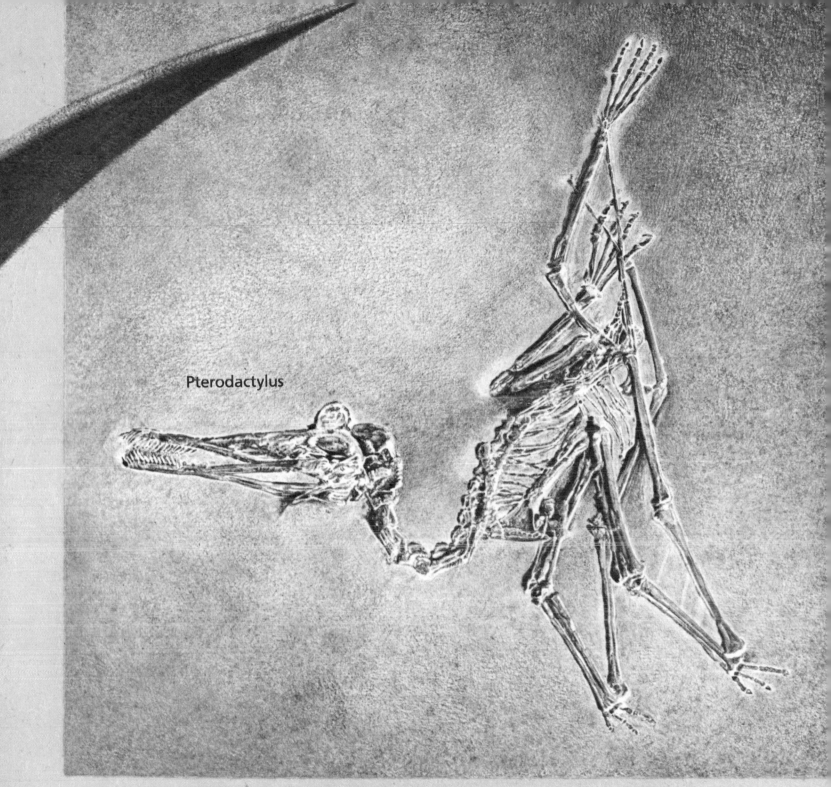

Pterodactylus

Pterodactyloidea

Gradually, the rhamphorhynchoids were displaced by a second suborder. Pterodactyloids had few teeth or none at all, long faces, long necks, and short tails. The strange fifth toe, always present in rhamphorhynchoids, was much smaller or missing entirely, and the metacarpals (the bones between the wrist and fingers) of the wing were quite long. Generally, pterodactyloids were much more delicate than rhamphorhynchoids. *Pterodactylus* was a small pterodactyloid with an average wingspan of 20 inches (51 cm), although some species were much smaller. These little pterosaurs were quite common along Late Jurassic shores.

CROCODILIA

Mesosuchia

Mesosuchians are thought to represent an intermediate evolutionary position between the primitive protosuchians of the Triassic (page 33) and modern crocodiles.

The family Teleosauridae was adapted to life in the shallows of Jurassic seas. Teleosaurs' legs, especially their front ones, were short and their long jaws were lined with many slender teeth.

Steneosaurus

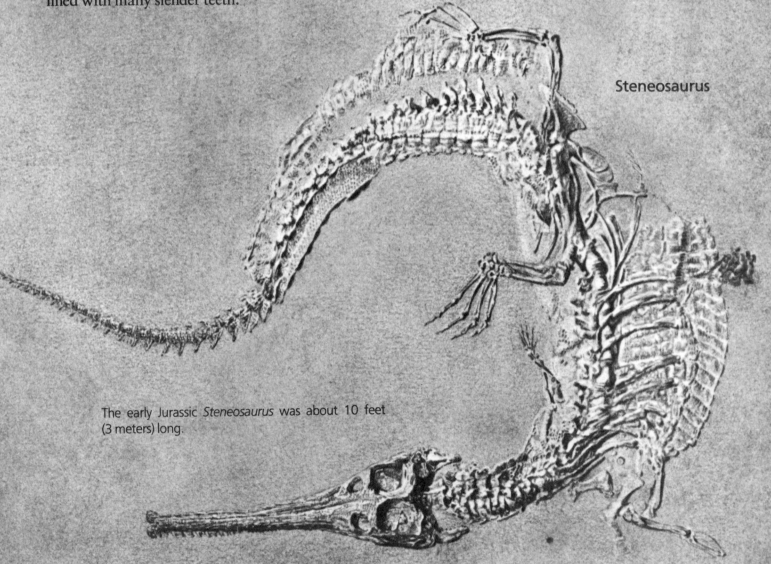

The early Jurassic *Steneosaurus* was about 10 feet (3 meters) long.

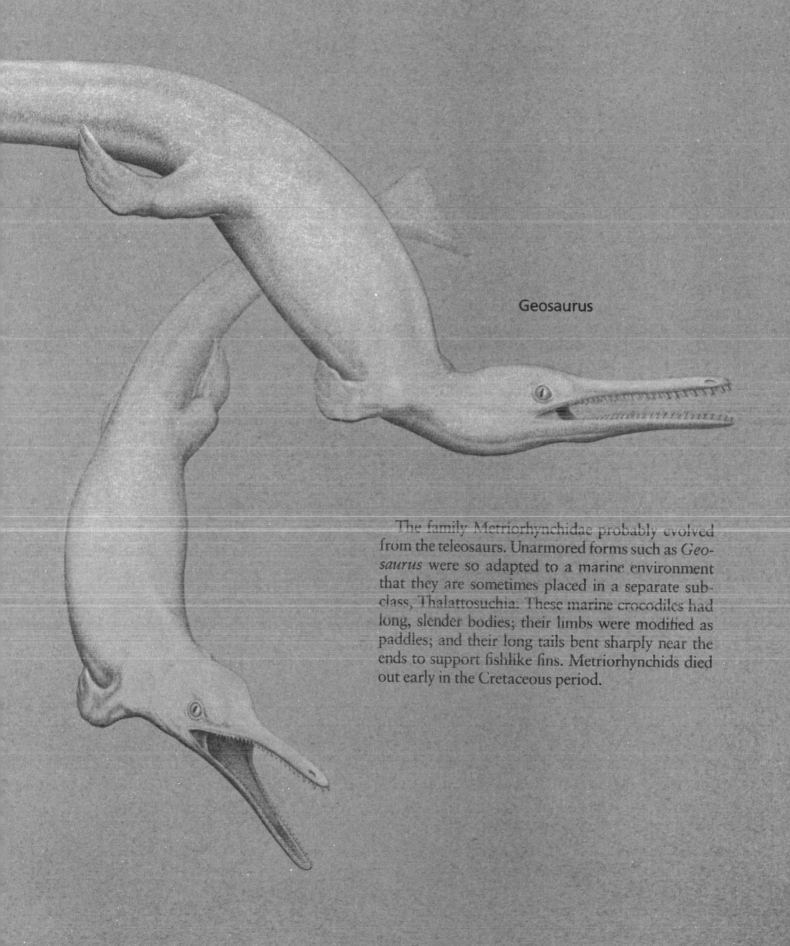

Geosaurus

The family Metriorhynchidae probably evolved from the teleosaurs. Unarmored forms such as *Geosaurus* were so adapted to a marine environment that they are sometimes placed in a separate subclass, Thalattosuchia. These marine crocodiles had long, slender bodies; their limbs were modified as paddles; and their long tails bent sharply near the ends to support fishlike fins. Metriorhynchids died out early in the Cretaceous period.

Cretaceous Period

THE THIRD AND longest period of the Mesozoic Era, the Cretaceous, lasted for about 70
million years—from 135 million to 65 million years
ago. Its name comes from *creta*, the Latin word for
"chalk," because chalky layers formed seabeds during this period.

During the Cretaceous, the continents continued
to separate (see the map on page 60). By the middle
of the period, Gondwanaland had broken apart: Africa moved toward its present position, while a large
land mass composed of Australia, India, and Antarctica moved to the southeast. Then India broke off and
began to drift to the north. Laurasia appears to have
remained intact until the Late Cretaceous, when the
supercontinent was subdivided by two shallow seas.
Eastern North America and Europe formed Euramerica. Asiamerica comprised western North America
and parts of Asia.

The incursion of the seas also separated South
America from the northern lands. Animals could no
longer move from continent to continent. In the
southern continents Cretaceous life was very similar
to that of the Jurassic. In the north, however, specifi-
cally in Asiamerica, tremendous changes were taking
place.

The climate, which was generally warm, grew
damper. Evergreens were gradually replaced by hard-
woods (including oaks, hickories, and magnolias) as
the dominant forest trees. Flowering plants multi-
plied and spread. As new kinds of plant life provided
a greater variety and quantity of food, entirely new
dinosaur groups evolved and flourished.

Except for the pterosaur *Quetzalcoatlus* (page 79) and the bird
Ichthyornis (page 69), all these animals are known from the Late
Cretaceous of Alberta, Canada.

As a pair of duck-billed *Parasaurolophus* look on, a horned
Monoclonius (page 77) fends off the tyrannosaur *Gorgosaurus*
while two *Struthiomimus* (page 64) flee. In the foreground are
the armored *Scolosaurus* (page 74) and *Dromaeosaurus* (page
64), a deinonychosaur.

Plant life included a variety of angiosperms (flowering plants).

59

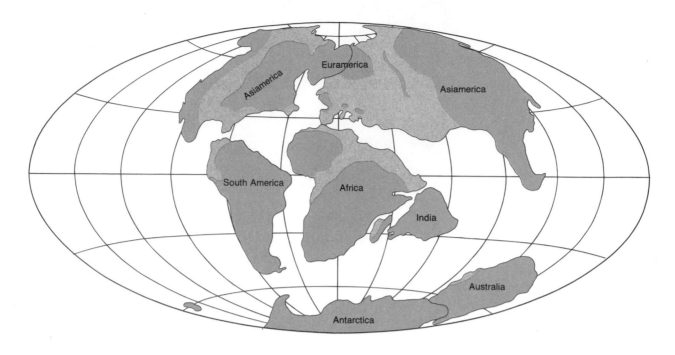

In Late Cretaceous time, about 90 million years ago, South America was an island and India had drifted northeast toward Asia. The continents were invaded by shallow seas (shown in blue).

Theropods

Many Cretaceous coelurosaurs were very similar in appearance to their Triassic and Jurassic ancestors. Others, the ornithomimids (bird imitators) for example, were graceful, fast, and some were fairly large. Many paleontologists assign ornithomimids to their own infraorder, Ornithomimosauria.

Deinocheirosaurs are known from a single specimen, a pair of hands, arms, and shoulderblades found in Mongolia. These bones are very similar to those of the ornithomimids but are so huge that they are relegated to their own infraorder, Deinocheirosauria.

A new group of theropods, the deinonychosaurs, arose in the Cretaceous. They were cunning, agile predators with excellent coordination and depth perception, and they probably hunted in packs. Certain skeletal features suggest that these small predators were closely related to *Archaeopteryx*—and that deinonychosaurs and birds shared a unique and common ancestor.

Infraorder Segnosauria was established in 1980 after the discovery in Mongolia of some lightly built flesh eaters whose pubic bones were parallel to their ischia (two of the hipbones). These animals are considered to be saurischians, in spite of this deviation from the hip structure with which the order is usually defined. Segnosaurs also lacked teeth in the front of their jaws, and their feet had four toes (each with a long claw), which all pointed forward.

The habits of the segnosaurs and their relationship to other theropods is not clear, but their discovery will cause some major revisions in our present system of classification.

Birds

The best known fossil Cretaceous birds were sea or shore birds. (Fossils, especially delicate ones such as those of birds and pterosaurs, are much more likely to be preserved in marine sediments than in terrestrial deposits.) Among the most interesting and best-known genera are the toothed birds.

Carnosaurs

The family Tyrannosauridae contains some of the most spectacular carnosaurs, culminating in the awesome genus *Tyrannosaurus*. This giant is the largest known terrestrial meat eater of all time.

An interesting family of carnosaurs, Spinosauridae, evolved in the Late Jurassic. Spinosaurs' dorsal vertebrae developed spines, which probably supported a sail-like structure similar to that found in the pelycosaur *Dimetrodon* (page 12). In Cretaceous spinosaurs, these sails grew progressively larger. In *Spinosaurus* some of these spines were more than 6 feet (1.9 meters) long.

Sauropodomorphs

The best-known and most spectacular sauropods are from the Jurassic period. Cretaceous sauropods differed in detail (one Cretaceous genus was even armored) but not in general from their Jurassic ancestors. Although the "brontosaurs" survived until near the end of the Cretaceous, they were replaced as the dominant plant eaters by the ornithischians of the Cretaceous.

Ornithischians

Several new families of ornithischian bipeds developed during the Cretaceous. The largest and best known is Hadrosauridae. The "duckbills" are known throughout Cretaceous Laurasia and probably descended from iguanodont stock.

Hadrosaurs (pages 70–71) were generally large, up to 40 feet (12.4 meters) long, and there was little difference among them in skeletal structure. The front ends of their jaws were flattened into ducklike bills. Behind the horny bill was a complex dental battery, in later genera often comprising hundreds of teeth. The tail was flattened laterally, and fossils show that the fingers were webbed, suggesting a semiaquatic existence. However, fossilized stomach contents show that hadrosaurs ate pine needles, cones, and twigs.

Recently, nests containing young hadrosaurs *(Maisaura)* were found in Montana. The evidence suggests that hadrosaurs took care of their young until well after hatching, and that hadrosaur social organization was much more complex than that of modern reptiles.

Pachycephalosaur (pages 72–73) fossils are rare and fragmentary. "Dome heads" were rather unspecialized bipeds; their skull roofs were thickened into helmets of solid bone. Some paleontologists feel that pachycephalosaurs should not be included in Order Ornithopoda, but should form their own suborder.

Troödon had been known for nearly a century from a few small, pointed, serrated teeth. In 1979 and 1980 more such teeth were found, as well as a jaw that apparently contained a predentary. *Troödon* is currently being evaluated to determine if it was in fact a carnivorous ornithischian. No other ornithischian carnivores have ever been found.

The stegosaurs disappeared around the end of the Jurassic, but another suborder of quadrupeds was evolving to replace them. The ancestry of the ankylosaurs (armored dinosaurs) is unknown.

A variety of ceratopsians (horned dinosaurs) evolved late in the Cretaceous period. Most were large and heavily built with huge skulls, parrotlike beaks, and long jaws lined with cutting teeth. These dinosaurs walked on all fours. The main difference among the various ceratopsians involved the pattern of horns, as well as the size and shape of the bony frill at the back of the skull.

Pterosaurs

The flying reptiles of the Cretaceous include the world's largest flying animals. Fossils of *Pteranodon* show wingspans of more than 25 feet (7.8 meters). In 1972 pterosaur remains were found in Big Bend National Park in Texas. They consisted of a complete and a nearly complete arm bone and several fragments of wing bones. Extrapolations from the measurements of smaller fossils found nearby and believed to be of the same genus put this pterosaur's wingspan at 36 feet (11 meters).

Crocodiles

Modern crocodiles, Suborder Eusuchia, appeared early in the Cretaceous, and by the end of the period the families Alligatoridae and Crocodylidae were well established in Laurasia.

Mesosuchians persisted through the Cretaceous. In fact, some genera might have survived in Australia until a million years ago. Cretaceous mesosuchians occurred in a variety of sizes, from around a foot (30 cm) to more than 35 feet (10.9 meters) long, and they occupied a greater variety of habitats than their modern relatives, today's crocodiles.

THEROPODA

Deinonychosaurs

In 1964, Dr. John Ostrom discovered in Montana the fossil of a theropod with a very unusual foot. Only two of its four toes (the third and fourth) were used for standing and running. Its second toe, which was shorter and raised above the ground, bore a lethal, sickle-shaped claw. Dr. Ostrom named this dinosaur *Deinonychus,* meaning "terrible claw."

Deinonychus was 8 to 9 feet (2.5 to 2.8 meters) long, weighing 175 to 200 pounds (79 to 90 kilograms). Its body was highly specialized for swift movement and savage attack. During an attack it slashed its prey with one hind foot while standing on the other. This kind of behavior required good coordination, excellent eyesight, a large brain, and a high level of energy—all associated with warm-blooded animals. Deinonychosaurs hunted in packs, cooperating to attack larger plant eaters.

Deinonychus

Bony rods (in orange) up to 30 inches (75 cm) long stiffened the long tail of *Deinonychus* so that it could use the tail for balance during agile movements.

In a fossilized foot of *Deinonychus*, the sickle-shaped bone is more than 3 inches (8 cm) long. In life it was covered by a knife-like sheath, producing a savage, 5-inch (13-cm) claw.

Deinonychus could turn its long, powerful hands toward each other. The hands could hold the prey to be slashed by one or both sharp-clawed feet.

THEROPODA

Ornithomimosaurs

Many Cretaceous coelurosaurs resembled their predecessors. But in the Late Cretaceous a new family developed in Asiamerica: the ornithomimids. Because of differences from the coelurosaurian pattern, some scientists would like to establish a new infraorder, Ornithomimosauria.

The ornithomimids resembled modern flightless birds (pages 90–91) but had long tails, long arms, and long, grasping fingers. Lacking sharp teeth, they may not have eaten meat exclusively.

Struthiomimus

Dromaeosaurus

Struthiomimus, the "ostrich mimic," was about 12 feet (3.7 meters) long and slightly taller than today's ostrich. Running on its three-toed feet, it could probably outpace small, fierce deinonychosaurs such as *Dromaeosaurus.*

Deinonychosaurs

Saurornithoides was a small meat eater found in Mongolia. Its huge, wide-set eyes provided excellent vision and depth perception. This large-brained, dexterous little creature may have preyed on tiny mammals, possibly nocturnal ones, such as *Zalambdalestes*.

Saurornithoides

Zalambdalestes

Tyrannosaurus

Carnosaurs

A new family of carnosaurs, Tyrannosauridae, arose in Asiamerica during the Late Cretaceous. *Tyrannosaurus* was more than 40 feet (12.4 meters) long, 10 feet (3 meters) high at the hips, and weighed around 5 or 6 tons (4.5 to 5.4 metric tons). Its primary weapons were the large talons on its massive hind limbs and the 6-inch (15-cm) recurved fangs that lined its 4-foot (1.2-meter) jaws. The forelimbs were disproportionately short but well muscled and ended in pairs of large claws. However, *Tyrannosaurus* couldn't even reach its mouth with its hands. Although it is usually pictured as an active hunter, some scientists feel *Tyrannosaurus* was too large and clumsy for this role. It might have been a scavenger.

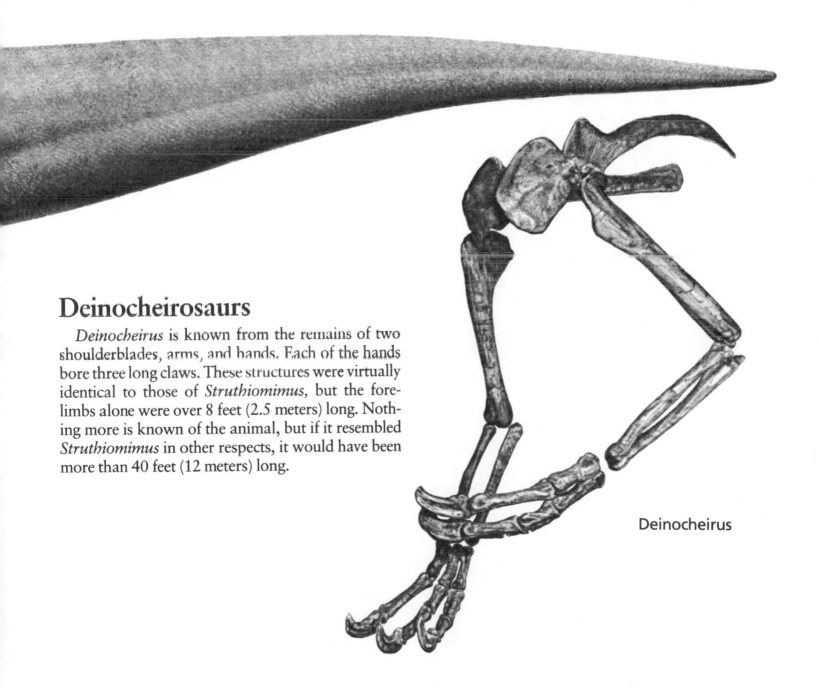

Deinocheirosaurs

Deinocheirus is known from the remains of two shoulderblades, arms, and hands. Each of the hands bore three long claws. These structures were virtually identical to those of *Struthiomimus*, but the forelimbs alone were over 8 feet (2.5 meters) long. Nothing more is known of the animal, but if it resembled *Struthiomimus* in other respects, it would have been more than 40 feet (12 meters) long.

Deinocheirus

Odontognathae

Hesperornis and *Ichthyornis* are usually classified together in the superorder Odontognathae because both of these Late Cretaceous birds had teeth. *Hesperornis* was a diving bird about 3.5 to 4 feet (about a meter) long. It had no keel-shaped ridge on its breastbone, its shoulder girdle was weak, and the wing was reduced to a single bone (humerus). *Hesperornis* certainly could not fly, and its legs were so specialized for its aquatic way of life that it must have had difficulty moving about on land.

Hesperornis

Ichthyornis

Ichthyornis was a strong flier. The skeleton shows the deep, keeled breastbone, strong shoulder girdle, and substantial wing bones needed for flight. Except for its teeth, it was much like modern birds, probably a fish eater, and lived like today's terns. Skeletal remains have been found in Kansas, which was covered by a shallow sea when *Ichthyornis* lived.

ORNITHOPODA

The Late Cretaceous of Asiamerica was populated by a huge community of hadrosaurs. Only the most primitive, Early Cretaceous subfamily has been found in Euramerica and Gondwanaland.

Corythosaurus

Saurolophus

There were many sorts of hadrosaurs. Generally they weren't very different but there were extraordinary variations in detail. Perhaps the most interesting of these differences is found in the various skull shapes. The crested Hadrosauridae fall into two groups. The solid-crested subfamily is small, comprising only five genera. *Saurolophus* had a solid crest.

In the larger subfamily, the crest contained long, often convoluted nasal passages. This development might have improved the animal's sense of smell or amplified its voice. *Corythosaurus* was a hollow-crested hadrosaur. *Anatosaurus*, a genus of the flat-headed variety, was one of the most successful and last surviving members of the family.

Anatosaurus

ORNITHOPODA

The pachycephalosaurs, or dome-headed dinosaurs, apparently were habitual bipeds with extremely thick skull roofs, studded with bony knobs. The skull of *Pachycephalosaurus*, the larger of the two established genera, was 2 feet (60 cm) long and capped with a dome of solid bone 9 to 10 inches (25 cm) thick. *Stegoceras* was a good deal smaller, only 6 to 7 feet (1.9 to 2.2 meters) long. The few well-documented fossils of this group are from Late Cretaceous Asiamerica. Scientists think that male pachycephalosaurs might have butted each other like modern rams to establish dominance during mating or territorial disputes.

Stegoceras

Skull of *Pachycephalosaurus*

ANKYLOSAURIA

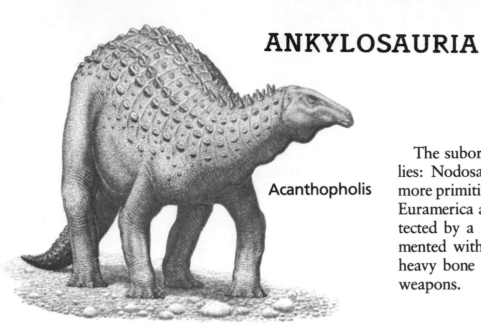

Acanthopholis

The suborder Ankylosauria comprises two families: Nodosauridae and Ankylosauridae. Only the more primitive nodosaurids have been found in both Euramerica and Asiamerica. Ankylosaurs were protected by a mosaic of bony plates sometimes augmented with sharp spikes. The tails of some bore heavy bone bludgeons, which must have served as weapons.

Acanthopholis was a primitive nodosaurid known from scattered fossil fragments in England.

Scolosaurus

Scolosaurus was a large ankylosaurid from Late Cretaceous Alberta, Canada.

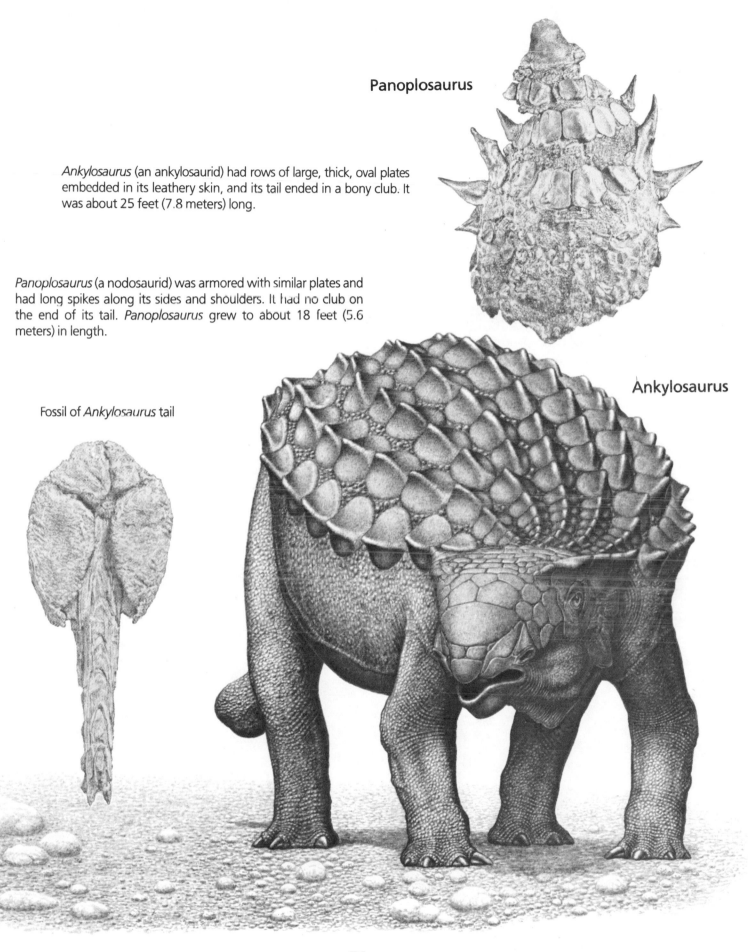

Panoplosaurus

Ankylosaurus (an ankylosaurid) had rows of large, thick, oval plates embedded in its leathery skin, and its tail ended in a bony club. It was about 25 feet (7.8 meters) long.

Panoplosaurus (a nodosaurid) was armored with similar plates and had long spikes along its sides and shoulders. It had no club on the end of its tail. *Panoplosaurus* grew to about 18 feet (5.6 meters) in length.

Ankylosaurus

Fossil of *Ankylosaurus* tail

Triceratops

The last ornithischian suborder to evolve was Ceratopsia (horned dinosaurs). They are all from Late Cretaceous Asiamerica.

Psittacosaurus

Monoclonius was about 20 feet (6 meters) long.

Monoclonius

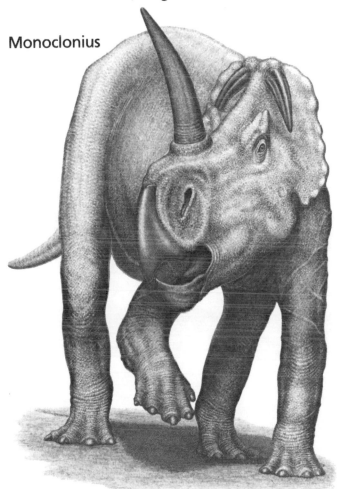

Psittacosaurus, because it occasionally walked on its hind feet, is often classified with the ornithopods. But many scientists believe that *Psittacosaurus* was more closely related to the ancestors of the ceratopsians. It was 6 to 7 feet (1.9 to 2.2 meters) long.

Protoceratops is the earliest ceratopsian dinosaur recognized by all scientists. It was 6 to 7 feet (1.9 to 2.2 meters) long.

Protoceratops

The best known of the horned dinosaurs is *Triceratops*. This huge ceratopsian grew up to 30 feet (9.3 meters) long and probably weighed about 6 tons (5.8 metric tons).

Triceratops was so large and so well equipped for defense that it is difficult to imagine how even *Tyrannosaurus* could have brought it down.

Large herds of *Triceratops* roamed western North America near the end of the Cretaceous.

77

PTEROSAURIA

Pterodactyloidea

The Cretaceous pterosaurs belong to the suborder Pterodactyloidea. They were less common than their Jurassic counterparts, presumably because of competition from birds. However, there were some remarkable types, including the largest animals ever to fly.

The general tendency seems to have been an increase in size without a corresponding increase in weight. *Pteranodon* attained wingspans of more than 25 feet (7.8 meters) yet might have weighed as little as 20 to 30 pounds (9 to 14 kilograms).

Crests were common among pterodactyloid genera, and in some species of *Pteranodon* a crest doubled the length of the toothless skull. Wind-tunnel tests show that the crest might have been an effective rudder in flight.

Pteranodon

Some large pterosaurs apparently did quite well without a crest. In 1972 remains of a giant Cretaceous pterosaur were found in Big Bend National Park, Texas. *Quetzalcoatlus'* wingspan has been conservatively estimated at 36 feet (11 meters).

Quetzalcoatlus

CROCODILIA

Eusuchia

Deinosuchus was a huge eusuchian (family Crocodylidae) known from Late Cretaceous North America and Europe. This illustration is based on the skull reconstruction at the American Museum of Natural History in New York City. The head alone was probably 6 feet (1.9 meters) long.

Deinosuchus

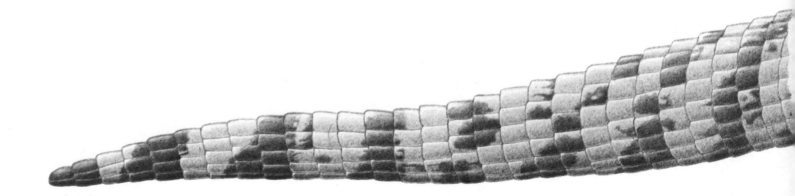

Various species attributed to the genus *Leidyosuchus* made up much of the crocodilian population of western North America during the Late Cretaceous and Early Cenozoic. There is such a large diversity of specimens grouped together in the genus *Leidyosuchus* that some paleontologists suggest further divisions on the generic level must be made.

The species illustrated is known from a number of fossils from North Dakota. The animal was a large, long-snouted eusuchian, which apparently ate fish. However, its rather long forelimbs and heavy armor suggest that it spent more time on dry land than today's crocodiles.

Leidyosuchus

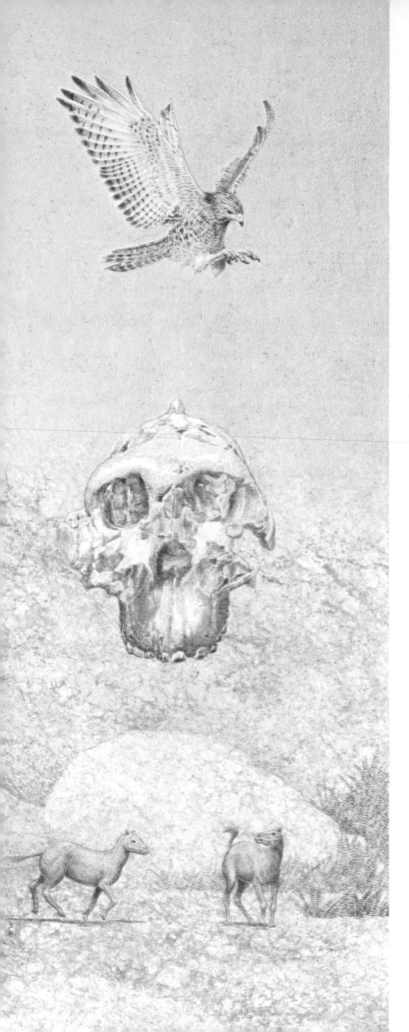

Cenozoic Era

THE CENOZOIC ERA, the Age of Mammals, is divided into two periods: the Paleogene and the Neogene (see the chart on the next page).

Paleogene plants were predominantly of modern genera but differed in species. Many Neogene specimens are identical to today's species.

Throughout most of the Paleogene, areas that now lie in cool, temperate zones were warmer and wetter. The Paleogene climate was more equable over the face of the earth. Fossils of crocodiles and a variety of subtropical trees, including palms, have been found in latitudes that would prohibit their growth today. Northern Alaska, Greenland, and Siberia supported forests of large redwoods, elms, oaks, walnuts, and other trees that require a moderately moist, temperate climate. Fossil leaves of magnolias and fig trees have been found in Paleogene deposits of Alaska. However, scattered glacial deposits are also known from this time, seemingly induced by the formation of mountains, which cause disturbances in the atmosphere and create precipitation.

At different times in the Paleogene, shallow seas covered many areas that are now dry land.

In the Neogene, temperatures gradually declined and large land areas cooled and dried. Another incursion of the seas took place in the Neogene, although the submerged areas were in quite different locations from those of the Paleogene. Gradually the seaways receded. At times during the last 2 million years of the Neogene, vast sheets of ice covered much of the earth's surface.

This illustration shows reconstructions of *Diatryma*, a large carnivorous bird (page 86), and *Oxyaena*, a flesh-eating mammal (creodont), about to attack a small herd of *Hyracotherium*, the dawn horse.

Framed in the huge tusk of the woolly mammoth skeleton is an impression of a dogwood leaf. The insect preserved in amber is *Sphecomyrma*, a transitional form between ants and wasps. The skull is *Zinjanthropus*, a hominid nearly 2 million years old.

In the air are a modern bat and a red-shouldered hawk.

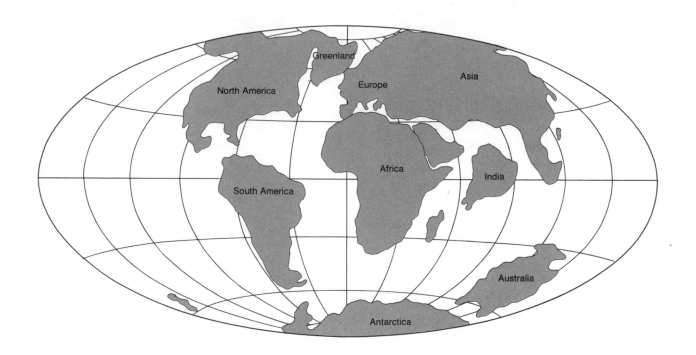

By the Cenozoic Era, 45 million years ago, India had crossed the Equator on its way to Asia, Africa and had moved closer to Europe, and Australia had split away from Antarctica.

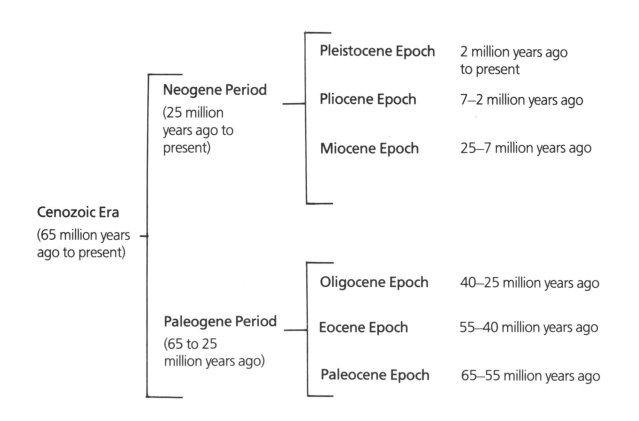

Animals of the Paleogene Period

Mass extinctions at the end of the Cretaceous left large gaps in the earth's ecology. A variety of Paleogene mammals gradually adapted themselves for many of the modes of life vacated by Mesozoic reptiles. The Paleogene showed specialization in teeth and limbs, and although it is considered the period of archaic mammals, the ancestors of most modern mammals can be traced back to the Paleogene.

Evolution of man may even be traced back to the appearance of primitive Paleogene primates. Ancestral primates were alert, tree-dwelling mammals with good binocular vision. Their digits were adapted for grasping and their joints for limb rotation. Slow postnatal development required extended parental care. Their anatomical features and life style fostered the evolution of higher levels of intelligence.

Approximately half of the orders of living birds can be traced back to the Paleocene and Eocene epochs, which together lasted from the end of the Cretaceous until about 40 million years ago. Large parts of North America and Europe were tropical during this time. The Atlantic and Indian oceans formed, and the Rocky Mountains were built. Most fossil birds from this period are of carinate orders (pages 88–89), possessing the keeled breastbone (carina) that allows for flight.

Gavials (members of the third family of modern crocodiles) first appear in the Paleocene fossil record.

Nearly all of the remaining carinate orders are represented in the Oligocene, which lasted from about 40 to 25 million years ago. This was a warm, dry period of continued mountain building, characterized by an increase of grasslands and a decrease in forests. Mammals continued to specialize during this epoch, and more modern forms evolved.

Animals of the Neogene Period

The Miocene Epoch began about 25 million years ago and lasted until 7 million years ago. The Alps and Himalayas formed during this time. The Miocene shows the greatest variety of mammals, and it was then that they achieved the greatest size. About 40 percent of Miocene birds belonged to modern genera.

During the Pliocene Epoch, which lasted until about 2 million years ago, mountain building slowed and the earth's surface stabilized. The Pliocene was cooler than the Miocene but still warmer than today. More than 70 percent of Pliocene birds were of modern genera.

Whereas nearly all of the carinate orders can be traced back to the Paleogene period, fossils of modern ratite groups go back only to the Pliocene. Ratites lack the keeled breastbones found in carinates and cannot fly. The absence of older ratite fossils might be attributed to their inland habitats. Animals that live near the shore are much more likely to be preserved than those that live inland.

The Pleistocene Epoch, which we live in today, has been punctuated by a series of ice ages, four of which were severe. The last ended about 10,000 years ago. These ice ages affected both plant and animal life, reducing the number of species and restricting their locales.

CLASS AVES

Diatrymiformes

The Eocene in North America and Europe produced a number of large, flightless, carnivorous birds that competed with the flourishing mammal population. *Diatryma* was a 7-foot-tall (2.2-meter) predator from the Early Eocene in Wyoming. No Post-Eocene Diatrymiformes have been found. Because of their possible relationship to the rails, Diatrymiformes are often included in Order Gruiformes.

Diatryma

Phororhacos

Throughout most of the Cenozoic, North and South America were unconnected. Large, placental mammals were absent on the southern continent and powerful, flightless, carnivorous birds evolved there in the absence of mammalian competition. They are classified with the Gruiformes and are thought to be closely related to the cariamas. *Phororhacos* was about 5 feet (1.6 meters) tall and had an 18-inch (46-cm) skull.

Phororhacos

Cariama

CLASS AVES

Falconiformes
vultures, hawks

Strigiformes
owls

Piciformes
woodpeckers, toucans

Spheanisciformes
penguins

Gaviiformes
divers (loons)

Galliformes
pheasants, fowls

Cuculiformes
cuckoos, roadrunners

Columbiformes
pigeons

Neognathae

The carinates are distinguished by the possession of structures evolved for flight. The carina is the large, keeled breastbone to which major flight muscles are attached.

Primary flight feathers are attached to the bones of the hand, which comprise several wristbones and three fingers. Secondary flight feathers attach to the ulna bone of the "forearm."

The larger bones are nearly all pneumatic, hollow with little marrow. Many are filled with air sacs, which connect to the lungs and increase the speed with which oxygen is replaced in the blood.

Birds' eyes are highly evolved, much more so than those of mammals, and show a variety of specializations related to their life style.

Today's carinates range in size from tiny hummingbirds little more than an inch (2.5 cm) long to large condors with wingspans of 12 feet (3.7 meters). However, some fossil forms are much larger.

Trogoniformes
trogons

Coraciiformes
rollers, hornbills, kingfishers

Psittaciformes
parrots

Passeriformes
perching birds

Apodiformes
hummingbirds, swifts

Caprimulgiformes
goatsuckers, nightjars

Coliiformes
colies

Pelecaniformes
pelicans

Charadriiformes
gulls, auks, waders

Gruiformes
cranes, rails

Ciconiformes
herons, storks,
flamingos*

Procellariiformes
albatrosses, petrels

Anseriformes
ducks, geese, swans

Podicipediformes
grebes

*Flamingos are sometimes classified separately in Order Phoenicopteriformes.

CLASS AVES

Paleognathae

Many scientists classify tinamous with the living ratites (ostriches, rheas, emus, cassowaries, and kiwis) and the extinct ratites (elephant birds and moas) in the superorder Paleognathae.

Tinamous are robust ground birds from South America. Although they retain some ability to fly, their skulls are similar to those of ratites.

In the absence of mortal enemies, birds evolve to improve their locomotion, nesting, and feeding habits on the ground and will sometimes even sacrifice their ability to fly. Scientists agree that ratites

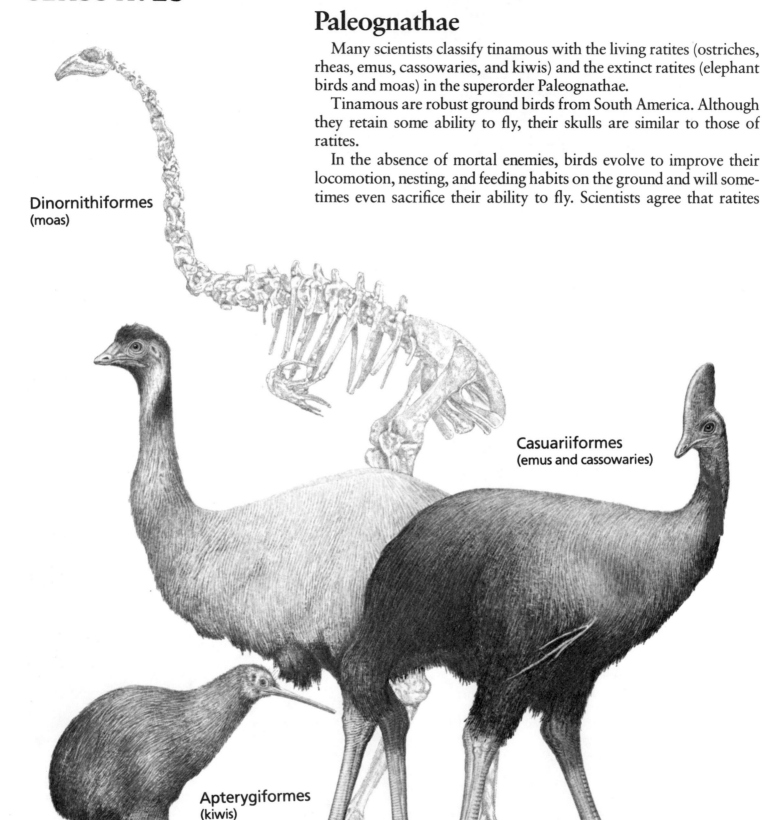

Dinornithiformes
(moas)

Casuariiformes
(emus and cassowaries)

Apterygiformes
(kiwis)

evolved from flying birds, but many doubt that ratites share a common ancestor. They feel that the ratites' common features are the normal response to ground dwelling and therefore are the result of convergent evolution.

Kiwis are found in New Zealand, and emus live in Australia. Cassowaries live in New Guinea and northern Australia. Rheas are confined to South America. Ostriches are now found only in Africa and Arabia, but they once roamed throughout southeastern Europe and Asia.

Aepyornithiformes
(elephant birds)

Struthioniformes
(ostriches)

Rheiformes
(rheas)

Tinamiformes
(tinamous)

GLOSSARY

Archosauria A superorder of reptiles. The "ruling reptiles" included thecodonts, dinosaurs, pterosaurs, and crocodiles.

Asiamerica The name given to the large land mass, composed of western North America and parts of Asia, that existed during the Cretaceous period.

Aves The class of vertebrates containing all the birds.

biped An animal that stands and walks on two legs.

carinate A bird that possesses a carina, the keeled breastbone to which powerful muscles usually associated with flight are attached.

carnivore A meat eater.

continental drift The theory that the surface of the earth is made up of several independent plates and is constantly changing as those plates (and therefore the land masses they support) move in relation to one another.

convergent evolution The process by which unrelated organisms evolve similar structures to perform similar functions in the same environment.

crest A natural growth on the top of an animal's head.

cusp Any prominence or point on the biting or chewing surface of a tooth.

dental battery A complicated arrangement of teeth, often interlocking and overlapping, that forms a highly effective unit.

dentaries The bones in the lower jaws that support teeth. In mammals, the dentaries form the entire lower jaw.

dentition The kinds, number, and arrangement of teeth.

Dinosauria ("terrible lizards") Sir Richard Owen's original name for a group of reptiles that now comprise the orders Saurischia and Ornithischia. Also, one of the names proposed for a new class of vertebrates that would contain Saurischia, Ornithischia, and the present class Aves (birds).

dorsal Pertaining to the back.

ectothermy Reliance on an external heat source (the sun) to raise the body's temperature.

endothermy The ability to generate heat internally by chemical means.

Euramerica The name given to the large land mass, composed of parts of North America and Europe, that existed during the Cretaceous period.

evolution The process by which the characteristics of a type of organism gradually change over a series of generations. Those best adapted to the prevailing conditions survive to perpetuate their kind.

fossil The preserved remains of an ancient organism or evidence of its existence. Fossilization usually involves the burial of the original material in sediments. Organic material may then be replaced by minerals.

fossil record The history of life on earth as revealed by fossils.

frill The term often used to refer to the flaring out of the back of the skull in ceratopsians.

furcula The "wishbone" in birds.

gizzard A prestomach or part of the stomach with muscular walls and a tough lining for churning and grinding food, sometimes with the aid of swallowed stones.

habitual Customary; tending to behave but not necessarily behaving in a certain way (as in "habitual biped").

herbivore A plant eater.

hominid A member of the family represented by the single genus *Homo* (man).

insectivore An insect eater.

metacarpals The bones of the hand between the wrist and the fingers.

nares The openings at each end of the nasal cavity. There are external nares (nostrils) and internal nares.

niche A position or type of environment particularly suitable for an organism.

nocturnal Active at night.

obligatory Referring to required behavior, as opposed to habitual behavior.

Ornithischia One of the two orders of dinosaurs. Ornithischia comprises at least four suborders: Ornithopoda, Stegosauria, Ankylosauria, and Ceratopsia.

paleontologist A scientist who studies fossils and attempts to reconstruct ancient organisms and determine their life styles and relationships to other organisms.

Pangaea The single land mass, made up of all the continents, that existed before and during part of the Triassic period.

pelvis The skeletal structure that rests on the legs and supports the spine. The bones that join with the head of the femur (thighbone) to form the hip.

placental Pertaining to the placenta, an organ in the reproductive system of some mammals that assists in the development of the unborn young. All surviving mammals have placentas except marsupials (pouched animals) and monotremes (egg layers).

pneumatic bones Hollow bones, filled during life with a lung sac, in certain birds and, perhaps, pterosaurs.

preadaptation The development of a structure in one environment that proves to be even more useful in another environment.

predator An animal that hunts and kills other animals (prey).

predentary The bone in ornithischian dinosaurs that joins the main jawbones to form the chin.

prey An animal hunted or killed for food by another animal (predator).

primates The most highly developed order of terrestrial mammals, including man, apes, monkeys, and lemurs.

process A bony projection.

quadruped An animal that stands and walks on four legs.

rails A group of small wading birds related to the cranes.

ratite A member of a group of ground birds that cannot fly because they have no keel on their breastbones.

recurved Curved backward.

Saurischia One of the two orders of dinosaurs. Saurischia comprises two suborders: Theropoda and Sauropodomorpha.

scavenger A carrion eater; an animal that eats decaying flesh or the flesh of a dead animal it hasn't killed.

scute An external horny or bony plate imbedded in the skin.

secondary palate The bone that forms the roof of the mouth separating the oral cavity from the nasal cavity.

serrated Notched along the edge like a saw.

specialization The process by which structures, organs, or organisms evolve or develop to perform a specific function or type of function.

terrestrial Pertaining to or confined to land as opposed to water or sky.

temperate Neither very hot nor very cold. Moderate.

temporal opening Openings in the sides of the skull behind the eyes.

tetrapod A vertebrate with four limbs; for example, amphibians, reptiles, mammals, and birds.

tuatara A lizardlike reptile found on islands off the coast of New Zealand. Tuataras are the last surviving members of an order that is very distantly related to lizards and snakes.

vertebra Any one of the bones that make up the spinal column.

vertebrate An animal with a backbone (Subphylum Vertebrata).

INDEX

Page numbers in *italic type* refer to illustrations.